Thirty walks from Brighton Station

Catching sights and sea air

John Twisleton

Illustrations by Rebecca Padgham

Commendations for
Thirty Walks from Brighton Station

Post Covid-19 habits have changed and we are now even more aware of the valuable green open spaces around us.

But where to go? Will we get lost? How long will they take? Canon John Twisleton has come up with the perfect solution to this frequent dilemma: Thirty Walks from Brighton Station and the greater Brighton area.

These local walks are all very well laid out giving simple directions and easy to follow maps by Rebecca, (but please still take your own) setting your walk before you step by step. These informative walks will give you the very simple pleasure of wellbeing while providing a great day out.

The volunteers at the award-winning Sussex Cricket Museum themselves formed a walking group, TMS (The Museum Strollers) during lockdown and I for one look forward to using some of these routes that John has so thoughtfully planned for all our pleasure.

I hope to meet some of you on these walks.

Phil Barnes

Sussex Cricket Museum Trustee

1

Father John is very familiar with the local area around Brighton and beyond and is an enthusiastic walker and explorer. One is in safe hands using this book as a guide. It combines his passion for walking with his knowledge of Brighton's landmarks and places of interest. I commend it to anyone who would like to become better acquainted with the city with its helpful insights, maps and range of walks. Whether one has a whole day to spend walking or just an hour to spare there is a great range of walks available as one sets off from Brighton Station on an adventure.

Father Ben Eadon CMP

Vicar of St Bartholomew, Brighton and St Paul, Brighton

An excellent publication, with easy to follow walking guidelines, plus an interesting description of the "sights" en route!

Mike Hedgethorne
Brightonian

Book cover showing Bungaroosh
'A composite building material used almost exclusively in the English seaside resort of Brighton and its attached neighbour Hove between the mid-18th and late 19th centuries, when it grew from a fishing village into a large town.' (Wikipedia)

Foreword

As a professional geographer and as a leader of walks and ambles in both urban and rural locations, I always have a penchant for books which direct fit and vigorous folk across hill and plain, or along 'mean streets' and elegant boulevards. Often I am left disappointed - geology is generally absent, even though it is the building block of all landscape, landscape is ignored or mis-understood, urban history, especially of Brighton, bowdlerised or even worse, plainly incorrect. When I had a sight of this volume, I was somewhat bemused as I initially thought 'he has bitten off more than he can chew' - a book which lists that number of walks - in the city, in the suburbs, in the rural hinterland - can only come to grief! However, this a competent creation. One difficulty that besets all walks leaders is getting participants to the same correct start point. This is not as unusual as it sounds. I once led a walk in Patcham that started at the Co-op store and was listed as such. A lost lady was waiting for me three miles away at a different Co-op store! These walks have the start point as Brighton Station and thus those from outside the city have a secure and undisputed meeting place. Having a wide range of walks of varying lengths allows for an eclectic suite of topics to be covered. It will be a superfit person to accomplish some of the longer forays into the local countryside, but they will have definite route instructions alongside a wide-ranging spread of facts and historical titbits. What struck me was the sheer enthusiasm of the writer and it shows a deep love of the topic and area.

Dr Geoffrey Mead
University of Sussex

Contents

Introduction

'Does this train stop at Brighton? I hope so or there's going to be a hell of a splash!' (Kenny Everett) Good walks from Brighton Station are more north, east and west than south on account of the sea. The old South Street of The Lanes is now underwater. Walking in Brighton is inspired yet limited by the seaside. 'Thirty Walks from Brighton Station - catching sights and sea air' is the fruit of my twenty year association with the city of Brighton & Hove including service on the City Forum 2001-9 and ongoing ministry as assistant priest at St Bartholomew's Church. Over that period my knowledge of sights has expanded from the popular duo of Pier and Pavilion to the two hundred and sixty six listed in this book.

Thirty walks are listed in rough order of length from one mile up to eighteen. All start from Brighton Station BN1 3XP. Twenty one walks are circular. Nine exploit public transport for the return journey. Detailed walk routes are provided alongside schematic illustrations which give the overall feel of each walk and its major sights. The circular walks head north through Brighton Greenway and Preston Park to Patcham, Stanmer House and Hollingbury Camp, east to The Level, Lewes Road Cemetery, Hanover, Queen's Park, Brighton Racecourse, Kemp Town, Brighton Marina and Ovingdean, west to St Ann's Well Gardens, Hove Park and Southease and south to North Laine, Royal Pavilion and Palace Pier. Other walks extend radially to Shoreham, Devil's Dyke, Chattri Memorial and Saltdean with longer excursions to Bramber Castle, Truleigh Hill, Jack & Jill Windmills, Ditchling Beacon, Lewes, Southease, Telscombe and Newhaven.

8

This book is the fruit of my romance with Brighton exploring her charm and diversity, her association with the sea and South Downs, her chequered history, creative present and future orientation. It is a practical handbook helping the reader get to places and appreciate the significance of the journeys and destinations. Drawing from sources including Clifford Musgrave's definitive 'Life in Brighton' this walk book inducts walkers en passant in the riches of local history. Today's city traces back to an age old fishing community transformed in the 18th century by Richard Russell's discovery of the curative power of sea-bathing. The Prince Regent (1811-1820) later King George IV stamped his mark on Brighton through building the Royal Pavilion finalised 1815-1822 by John Nash. With the railway's arrival in 1841 Brighton started to belong to everyone, chiefly day visitors, and became 'London-by-the Sea'. The resurgence of creative employment and ease of the commute north has more recently led to renaming London 'Brighton-inland'.

Communities get amnesia and cities with fast changing populations are prime candidates. Celebrating how we came to be where we are helps maintain a healthy community. Our sense of heritage builds our confidence as a community to face the future in a world that centres on the 'mini world' of family and 'mega world' of media often to the detriment of the 'midi world' of our locality. Walking around Brighton & Hove builds engagement with that locality, lowers our carbon footprint and helps us catch the sights and sea air. Most of the walks in this book are highly accessible since they are on pavements. More far-flung walks are on public footpaths bringing with that responsibility to respect surrounding land in private ownership especially farmland and to take special care when passing livestock.

The book provides acknowledgement of writings that inform it and in the same vein commends to readers the museums and libraries of Brighton & Hove. I would like to thank Brighton resident James Twisleton for his help and most especially Brighton based Rebecca Padgham for providing the illustrations.

'One has to be alone, under the sky, before everything falls into place and one finds one's own place in the midst of it all' wrote Thomas Merton. May such a grace be granted to all who take up this book and set themselves to explore Brighton & Hove and its surroundings.

Canon Dr John F Twisleton   **October 2022**

List of Sights

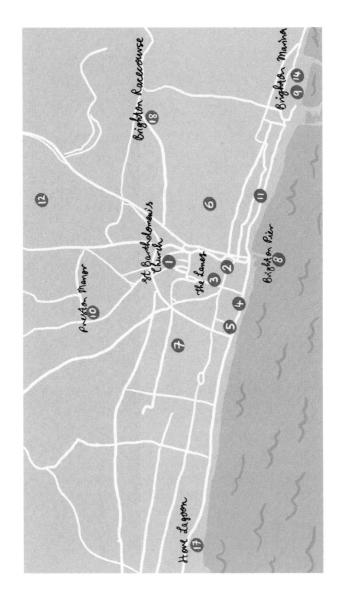

Map key: Brighton & Hove

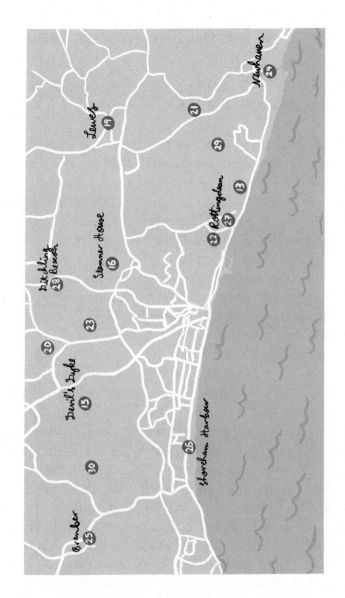

Map key: around Brighton & Hove

1   St Bartholomew's Church

1 mile circular walk to the tallest parish church in Britain returning via St Peter's Church

'I pushed open the door... and was quite overcome by its size and magnificence. There was a whole altar made of silver... and the high altar was so vast I imagined elephants might come in from either side and look like poodles. Along the sides were great confessional boxes which seemed like the Royal Pavilion had had puppies, and the Stations of the Cross were half life-size' Colin Stephenson (1). The Church of England is defined as 'the ancient church of this land, catholic and reformed' (Revised Catechism). Three centuries after the break with Rome the Oxford Movement was instrumental in recovering the catholic element of Anglicanism. The building of St Bartholomew's Church, 'Cathedral of Anglocatholicism', on Ann Street by Fr Wagner in 1874 in an Italian Gothic style is vivid demonstration of this recovery. Designed by local architect Edmund Scott and 135 foot (40 metres) tall, Bart's has the distinction of being the tallest parish church in Britain if not Europe. To this day visitors ask "is this a Roman Catholic Church?" to which the answer is, "No, it's not, it's Church of England!" As the church leaflet explains, Fr Wagner's vision included 'the promotion of the Christian faith in its catholic fullness, a single-minded commitment to the poor and vulnerable, and the promotion of education' (2). The adjacent school and choral tradition at Bart's serve these aims helping young and old access worship suited to the extravagance of the building.

Exiting the ticket barrier at Brighton Station turn left then left again past the cycle storage and taxi rank onto Stroudley Road. Descend the stairs and cross New England Street into Ann Street walking down past the primary school to the Church door. St Bartholomew's, nicknamed 'Noah's Ark', is manned by a welcoming team most days 10am-1pm details of which are at www.stbartholomewsbrighton.org.uk After visiting Bart's continue down to London Road and turn right along the pavement which enters York Place passing the recently restored St Peter's Church on the left which has a prominence on the main road to the pier complementing Bart's ascendancy near the station. Built 1824-8 St. Peter's is 'one of the first early nineteenth century churches to be built in the Gothic style... Barry's tower... built of dazzling white Portland stone, soars out of the valley of the Steine' (3). Turn right up Trafalgar Street to return to Brighton Station.

0.8 mile/1.3 km

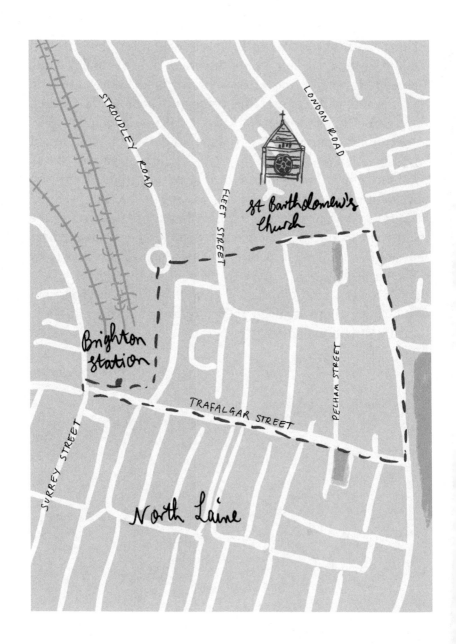

STROUDLEY ROAD

LONDON ROAD

FLEET STREET

St Bartholomew's Church

Brighton Station

PELHAM STREET

TRAFALGAR STREET

SURREY STREET

North Laine

2   Royal Pavilion

1 mile circular walk via North Laine to the Royal Pavilion returning via North Street

The Prince of Wales, later King George IV, first visited Brighton aged 21 in 1783. He came here to escape the scrutiny of London, seek the curative power of the sea and catch up with his dissolute uncle Henry, already resident. King George III's son contracted a romance with Maria Fitzherbert, marrying her secretly, forbidden to do so by Law as she was a Roman Catholic and he was heir to the throne. The Prince, from 1811 Prince Regent due to his father's decline, bought a farmhouse on Old Steine and enlarged it in neo-classical style as his palace to serve this liaison and their expanding social circle. Ongoing work on the new palace, including a riding school and stables, climaxed with John Nash's work 1815-22 creating the famous Indo-Islamic exterior with its large spherical dome and two pairs of smaller domes. The breath-taking restful lines of the eastern front are complemented by the less regular western front which embraces the picturesque gardens of the Royal Pavilion which in 1850 was sold by the government to Brighton Corporation for £50k. The Pavilion, open daily, is furnished with decorative works of art which help recreate its original splendour (4).

On leaving the station turn right at the forecourt. At the metal gate turn left following the railings down Trafalgar Street past Brighton Toy & Model Museum (closed Mondays) which also hosts Visitor Information. Cross to The Lord Nelson pub (1848) named by association with Trafalgar Street. On descending further St Bartholomew's Church comes into view down Whitecross Street to your left and the tower of St Peter's Church before you turn right at Sydney Street into North Laine. Continue past the Green Dragon pub. At the crossroads turn right along Gloucester Road then left down the pedestrianised Kensington Gardens. At the T junction with North Road turn right then left into Gardner Street passing Dorset Arms (1819) on your right. The Vegetarian Shoes shop is well known nationally. At Church Street turn left past Dockerill's Ironmongers (1915) still kept by the Dockerill family.

Take a right turn along New Road past the Unitarian Church (1820) with its facade modelled on the Temple of Theseus in Athens. Turn left before the Theatre Royal into Pavilion Gardens noting the statue of comedian Max Miller (1894-1965) in front of Brighton Dome, former stables of the Royal Pavilion, Georgian heart of Brighton. This is accessed by heading to the right across the gardens. Continue past the India Gate (1921) donated by the Maharajah of Patiala in commemoration of the wounded Indian soldiers tended in the Pavilion 1914-1915. At North

Street turn right passing the Chapel Royal. Continue and turn right up Bond Street. Head left up the ancient alley between numbers 14 and 15 into Jew Street recalling the town's early association with Jewry. At Church Street turn left then right into Tichborne Street where Brighton Buddhist Centre represents a more recent import of spiritual allegiance. Turn left into North Road and at Three Jolly Butchers pub (1865) right into Frederick Street. Turn right at Gloucester Road then left along Over Street to Trafalgar Street where you turn left under the railway bridge and right into Brighton station forecourt.

1.1 mile/1.8 km

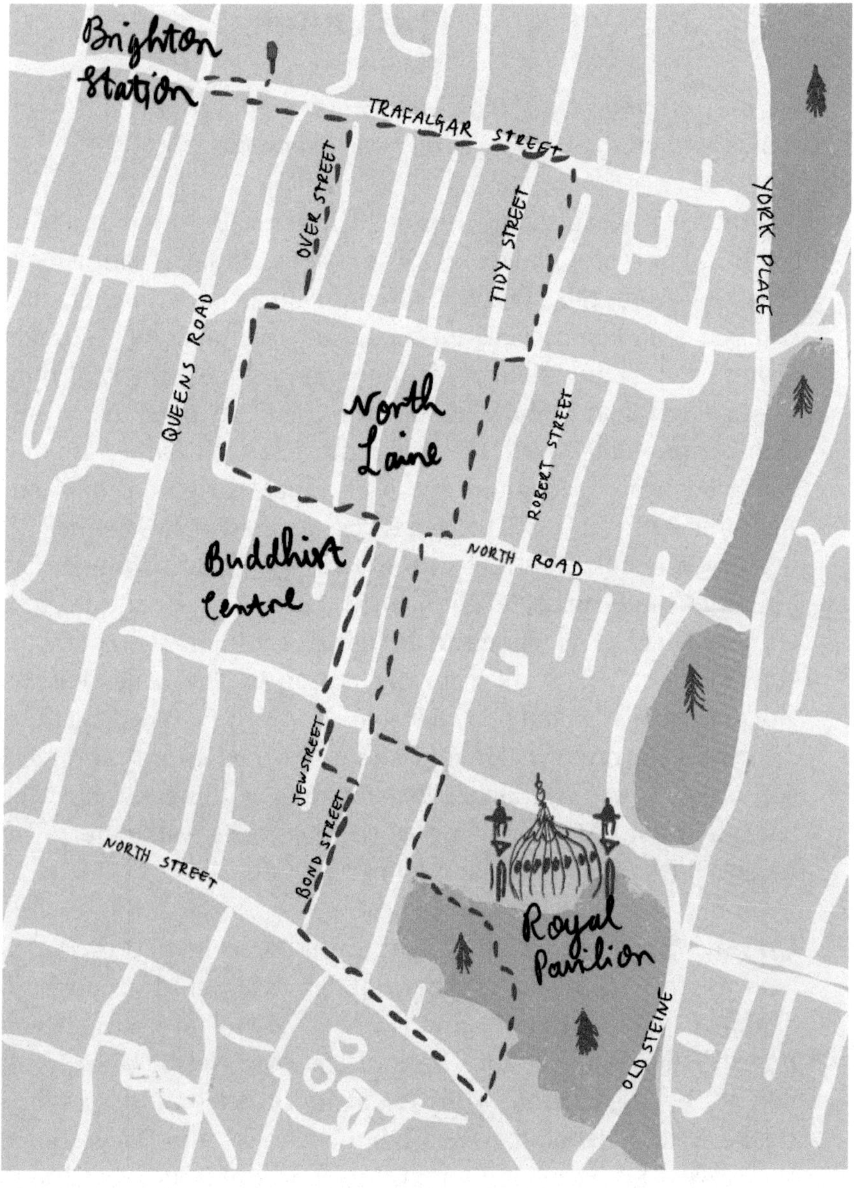

Brighton Station

TRAFALGAR STREET

OVER STREET

TIDY STREET

YORK PLACE

QUEENS ROAD

North Laine

ROBERT STREET

Buddhist Centre

NORTH ROAD

JEW STREET

BOND STREET

NORTH STREET

Royal Pavilion

OLD STEINE

3   The Lanes

1.5 mile circular walk via North Laine and Town Hall to The Lanes returning via Duke Street and Clock Tower

The narrow alleys in the centre of historic Brighton south of North Street are known as 'The Lanes' though confusingly accessed from the station by walking through 'North Laine' which has no historical connection. The original five great fields around the fishing village were tenantry 'Laines'. In 1738 they totalled 921 acres. Builders bought them up over the years. Densely populated over the last century, North Laine's unique character was recognised by Ken Fines, Brighton Borough Planning Officer (1974-1983). Fines persuaded the council to preserve the narrow streets, resist redevelopment with high rise buildings and institute the North Laine Conservation Area (1977). There is a plaque to Fines (d 2008) in the centre of North Laine. This walk from the station to The Lanes follows North Laine's mainly pedestrianised streets lined with a fascinating array of cafes and shops devoted to art, antiques, second-hand books, musical instruments, clothing and new age paraphernalia. After crossing North Street the walk enters The Lanes which exhibit similar commercial interests.

On leaving the station, turn right at the forecourt. At the metal gate turn left following the railings as you descend into Trafalgar Street past Brighton Toy & Model Museum which hosts Visitor Information. Cross to The Lord Nelson pub (1848) named by association with Trafalgar Street. On descending further St Bartholomew's Church comes into view down Whitecross Street to your left and the tower of St Peter's Church

31

before you turn right at Sydney Street into North Laines. At the crossroads turn right along Gloucester Road then left down pedestrianised Kensington Gardens. At the T junction with North Road turn right then left into Gardner Street passing Dorset Arms (1819) on your right. The Vegetarian Shoes shop is well known nationally. At Church Street turn right then left along Bond Street past the William the Fourth pub (1829). At the T junction with North Street turn left.

Cross the road at the pedestrian crossing to enter the passage straight ahead signed 'The Lanes' continuing under the Jubilee Arch (2002) straight along the alley to the Bath Arms (1864). In the cellar there is a bricked up tunnel connecting with a maze of underground passages under the Lanes. A former landlord was famed for his parrot which flew around the pub. Continue with Bath Arms to your right then left to The Lanes Armoury founded by Henry Hawkins (1920) and managed by his grandson Mark. Turn right past the jewellers' shops and Bohemia Grand Cafe onto Prince Albert Street. The Cricketers (1547) allegedly Brighton's oldest pub was a favourite of 'Brighton Rock' novelist Graham Greene. Take a detour left to view Brighton Town Hall (1832) built in Greek Revival Style. Return up Prince Albert Street past the Friends Meeting House into Ship Street and then left at the old Trinity Chapel along Duke Street. At the T junction turn right up West Street and cross North Street with the Clock Tower to your left walking up Queen's Road to Brighton Station.

1.4 mile/2.3 km

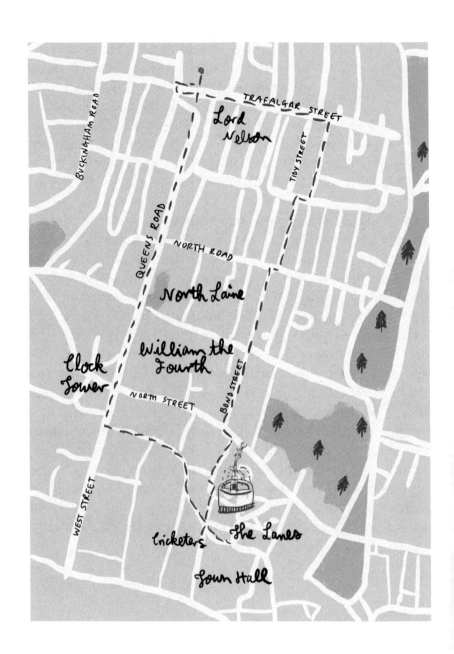

Buckingham Road

Trafalgar Street

Lord Nelson

Tidy Street

Queens Road

North Road

North Laine

William the Fourth

Clock Tower

North Street

Bond Street

West Street

Cricketers

The Lanes

Town Hall

4   Grand Hotel

2 mile walk via St Nicholas Church to The Grand Hotel returning via St Paul's Church

The Grand Hotel opened 1864 to cater as it still does for Brighton's richer visitors. Built on the site of a previous coastal fortification in Italian Renaissance style it was described as a 'cyclopean [undressed stone] pile with its nine tiers of rooms, with their elaborate ornamentation and bronzed and gilded balconies, from which visitors could luxuriate in the lovely panorama of sea and land that was spread to the view' (5). The Pump Room on the Promenade below was built at the same time as the hotel. Drinking Brighton's sea water was considered so beneficial every room in the Grand Hotel had three taps: one hot, one cold and a third for sea water pumped from below. On 12 October 1984 the Provisional Irish Republican Army bombed the hotel in an attempt to assassinate Prime Minister Margaret Thatcher who was attending the Conservative Party conference. Though Mrs Thatcher survived, five other people were killed. The priest from round the corner at St Paul's was summoned to pray before the conference opening, which was kept as planned the next day, at which Margaret Thatcher spoke in defiance of the bombers and won widespread admiration. 'The Grand' was reopened 28 August 1986 when Thatcher again spoke and the Concorde supersonic plane flew over to salute the reopening.

Go straight ahead on exiting the ticket barrier and turn right outside the station continuing to the pedestrian crossing. Cross and go straight up Guildford Road to the Battle of Trafalgar pub and turn left along Guildford Street. Cross Upper Gloucester

Road into Centurion Road. As the road turns left, continue along the passage to Mount Zion Place. Turn left then right into St Nicholas Churchyard walking around Brighton parish church, 14th century in origin but rebuilt 1854, continuing into Dyke Road. Turn left and then right along Upper North Street. Take the second left down Marlborough Street to Western Road. Cross into scenic Clarence Square descending into Russell Square. Turn left continuing to Cannon Place and then right walking down to King's Road on the seaside. The Grand Hotel is immediately on your left. Continue along King's Road then turn left up West Street to St Paul's Church accessed from the street via a long corridor. Continue up to the Clock Tower, erected 1888 to honour Queen Victoria's golden jubilee, and ascend from there back to the railway station.

1.7 mile/2.7 km

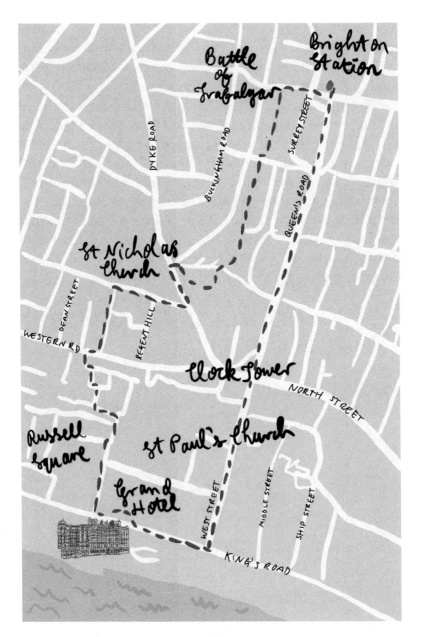

Battle of Trafalgar

Brighton Station

DYKE ROAD

BUCKINGHAM ROAD

SURREY STREET

QUEEN'S ROAD

St Nicholas Church

DEAN STREET

REGENT HILL

WESTERN RD

Clock Tower

NORTH STREET

Russell Square

St Paul's Church

Grand Hotel

WEST STREET

MIDDLE STREET

SHIP STREET

KING'S ROAD

37

5   Regency Square

2 mile walk via St Nicholas Rest Garden to Regency Square returning via i360 and Clock Tower

Brighton's transition to a spa resort was accompanied by so-called Regency architecture of neoclassical style. Discovery of the benefits of sea water was main agent. King George III reigned 1760-1820 and due to his infirmity his son, often resident in Brighton, acted as so-called Regent during the King's last 9 years. Regency Square was built to serve the need for housing from 1818 onwards on a site just outside historic Brighton previously favoured for fairs, shows and military reviews. These moved to The Level. Other notable local Regency or pre-Victorian (1837) buildings include Kemp Town and Hove's Brunswick Square. Oscar Wilde (1854-1900) once crashed his carriage in Regency Square dismissing the event as 'a matter of no importance'. Once used as an army camp, the grassed Square with its fine Regency housing now hosts an underground car park. It used to have immediate access to the defunct West Pier but is now dominated by the pier's vertical successor, the i360, which offers more extensive sea views. The 162 m (531 ft) observation tower on the seafront was opened by British Airways 2016 beside the remains of the West Pier. At the bottom of Regency Square the fine Royal Sussex Regiment War Memorial, surmounted by its bugler, is sadly dwarfed by i360.

Go straight ahead on exiting Brighton station ticket barrier and turn right outside the station continuing to the pedestrian crossing. Cross and go straight up Guildford Road to the Battle of Trafalgar pub (1805) and turn left along Guildford Street.

Cross Upper Gloucester Road into Centurion Road. As the road turns left, continue along the passage to Mount Zion Place. Turn right along Buckingham Road and walk past St Nicholas Church to Dyke Road. Cross into St Nicholas Rest Gardens bordered by a neat array of headstones and fourteen Grade II listed burial vaults with matching doors, one openable. On return to Dyke Road turn right and then right along Upper North Street heading for the spire of St Mary Magdalene Roman Catholic Church. Turn left down Spring Street, right along Hampton Street, left down Hampton Place and left along Western Road. Cross and descend Preston Street, with its fascinating variety of restaurants. Turn left to enter and view Regency Square and head down towards the i360. Turn left along the pavement of King's Road and walk past the Metropole Hotel (1890) and Grand Hotel (1864). Turn left after Brighton Centre (1977) to ascend West Street past St Paul's Church up to the Clock Tower where the walk concludes by ascending Queen's Road back to the railway station.

2.1 mile/3.3 km

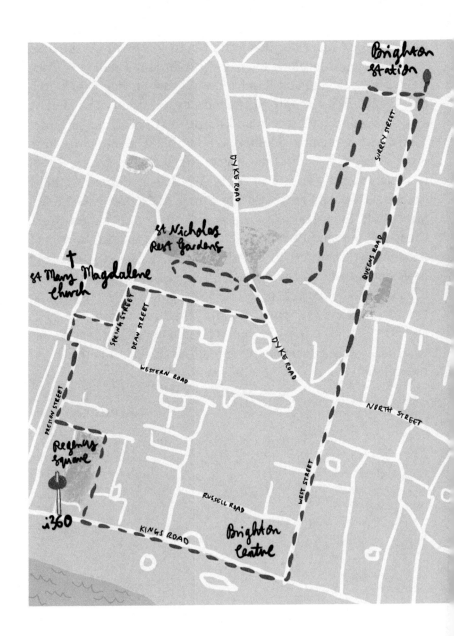

Brighton Station

SURREY STREET

DYKE ROAD

St Nicholas Rest Gardens

St Mary Magdalene church

SPRING STREET

DEAN STREET

WESTERN ROAD

DYKE ROAD

QUEENS ROAD

NORTH STREET

PRESTON STREET

Regency Square

i360

WEST STREET

RUSSELL ROAD

KINGS ROAD

Brighton Centre

6   Queen's Park

2.5 mile walk to Queen's Park via Hanover returning via Brighton Museum & Art Gallery

Well known to city residents but less known to visitors Queen's Park lies between Hanover and Kemptown with attractive grounds, pond, cafe and scented garden. To its south was the German Spa opened in 1825 by Dr Struve of Dresden for distribution of manufactured waters. The neoclassical remains of the Spa, which continued until 1960 as a mineral water plant, are now part of the Royal Spa Nursery school. Initially waters were dispensed from May to October every morning from 6am to 11am. Queen's Park was designed after Regent's Park in London and from the 1830s served the flow of Spa clients including Queen Adelaide, spouse of King William IV, whose name provided the Park title. This walk continues up the steep hill of Hanover, with narrow streets housing commuters and students, descending to the 'green sun trap' of Queen's Park and returns west via Brighton Museum & Art Gallery (1902) part of the Royal Pavilion estate, municipally owned and adjacent to Brighton Dome Concert Hall, the former royal stables. The 80 ft (24 m) cupola once covered a large lotus-shaped fountain used to water the horses.

Exiting the ticket barrier at Brighton Station turn left then left again past the cycle storage onto Stroudley Road. Descend the stairs and cross New England Street into Ann Street down to London Road. Cross into Oxford Street continuing from the Bat & Ball pub across Ditchling Road into The Level heading past the public toilets and Water Feature to the pedestrian crossing.

Cross the A270 turn left then right for a steep ascent up Southover Street into Hanover passing Phoenix Halls on your right, Annunciation Church on your left just down Washington Street and the Community Centre. At the mini roundabout turn half right up Montreal Road. Turn left down Albion Hill continuing across Queens Park Road to Queen's Park. Turn right then left down the slope where you can walk left to view the Park Monument then retrace your route to the metal gate by the trees. Turn left through the gate along the path which has a fine view of the Clock Tower. Turn right to continue along the lakeside and head for the South Road exit. Walk to the right down under the arch facing the Primary School and turn immediately right up Park Hill catching sight of the neoclassical edifice of Royal Spa Nursery School. At the top of the hill view the splendid main entrance to the Park. Walk in front of this across Queen's Park Road then left down Upper Park Terrace. Enjoy the sea view before continuing down Carlton Hill with the Greek Orthodox Church on your right and the rear of Brighton Police Station further down to the left. At Grand Parade turn left to the pedestrian crossing. Cross continuing left towards the Royal Pavilion to access Brighton Museum & Art Gallery. From the Museum return left up Church Street passing the Dome buildings and the Laine at the junction of Bond Street and Gardner Streets. At Queen's Road head right through Brighthelm Church and Community Centre gardens to cross North Road and walk up Queen's Road to Brighton Station.

2.3 mile/3.7 km

QUEEN'S PARK ROAD

ISLINGWORD ROAD

EWART STREET

Queen's Park

Greek Orthodox Church
+

Hanover

the Level

Brighton Museum & Art Gallery

FLEET STREET

NORTH ROAD

Brighton Station

QUEEN'S ROAD

45

7   St Ann's Well Gardens

2.5 mile circular walk via Brighton Mosque to St Ann's Well Gardens returning via St Michael's Church

As sea-bathing in Brighton developed in the 18th century interest grew in taking water more palatable than sea water as at St. Ann's Well in Hove. Visitors came to receive water drawn from the old chalybeate (iron-bearing) spring. 'Around 1800 an elaborate "pump room" was built over the spring, housing assorted facilities and accommodating the large numbers who came seeking therapeutic relief at that time... The Prince Regent's spouse Maria Fitzherbert wrote that "....the waters have wonderfully improved my health and strength." after a visit to the Spa in 1830. In 1882 the Brighton Gazette wrote that St. Ann's Well was 'one of the finest springs in Europe'. However, the distance of the Spa from Brighton, competition from other facilities, and a slow decline in the flow of the spring led to the spa's declining popularity, and it eventually closed... Because the spring's flow had slowed, the pump room was demolished in 1935, and a mock wellhead was installed in its place' (6). The link with Ann is allegedly based on the myth of Annafrieda, a Saxon lady whose tears of grief over the murder of her lover became the Chalybeate Spring. This walk presents a reminder of the hospitality of Brighton & Hove to minority groups. It passes the city's first Mosque founded in the late 1970s as well as Coptic, Anglican and Baptist Churches and a memorial in St Ann's Garden significant to the gay community. Whereas in many parts of the world minorities tolerate one another Brighton & Hove at its best aims at a respect for those who live differently going beyond tolerance. Respect, for example, given to Muslims, expressed in attendance by many non-Muslims in the daily breaking of fast during Ramadan. The Brighton & Hove Pride Festival in August is an internationally famous celebration of respect and diversity led by the LGBTQ+ community.

Exiting the ticket barrier at Brighton Station turn left then left again past the cycle storage and taxi rank onto Stroudley Road. Continue past the steps to enter Brighton Greenway which follows an old railway track. Descend to New England Road, turn right and continue right on the pavement up Old Shoreham Road (A270) past St Luke's Church (1875) to the crossroads. Turn right up Dyke Road and stop to view and maybe visit Brighton 'Alquds' Mosque. Continue briefly towards Dyke Road Park, cross and descend Crocodile Walk back to Old Shoreham Road. Cross the road, turn right and after a distance left down Montefiore Road continuing across Highdown Road to its junction with Davigdor Road. St Mary and St Abraam Coptic Orthodox Church (formerly St Thomas Anglican Church) faces you. Cross into the path to the left of the Church. At the bottom cross Nizells Avenue into St Ann's Well Gardens. Continue on the path in the same direction and turn right to walk in front of the Nursery and then left before the tennis court walking down to the LGB&T Suicide Memorial Tree. Continue to the wall behind this walking right and then left around the corner. Walk up to the tarmac path and reconstruction of St Ann's Well. Continue right to exit the Gardens into Furze Hill. Turn left and cross York Avenue into Temple Gardens where you see the classical facade of Brighton Girls School on the left. Continue across Vernon Gardens to view and maybe visit St Michael's Church (1862) on Victoria Road. Built in the

Italianate style, the stained glass windows are said to be the finest in Sussex. Turn left immediately after the Church up Powis Road to The Crescent Pub. Cross Clifton Hill and walk up Clifton Road. Turn right at Dyke Road then cross the road into West Hill Road passing West Hill Baptist Chapel. At the T junction turn right along Buckingham Road then left down Guildford Road past the Battle of Trafalgar Pub descending to the pedestrian crossing on Terminus Road. Cross here into the forecourt of Brighton Station.

2.4 mile/3.9 km

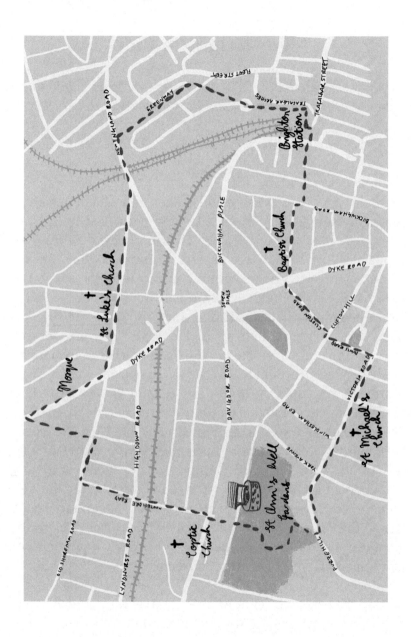

8   Brighton Pier

2.5 mile circular walk via West Street and Promenade to the Palace Pier returning via Royal Pavilion and Trafalgar Street

Ah, dear Brighton - piers, queers and racketeers. Noel Coward

London's love affair with Brighton traces back to the championing of sea bathing and sea air as healing remedies in the eighteenth century. Fuelled by royalty interest in Brighton grew so that a flow of up to 40 coaches a day grew from the capital leading to the arrival of the railway in 1841. Interest from the surge of visitors centred on accessing the sea so that the former wooden landing stages gave way to metal structures with a screw mechanism holding them down to the sea. Two piers were built at first, the Chain Pier (1823) reaching out 1,114 ft (340 m) and West Pier (1866) constructed a foot longer opposite Regency Square (7). They competed until a storm destroyed the first in 1896. The current Palace Pier, built between the two and longer than either at 1,710 ft (521 m), opened 1899 and was reconstructed 1911. The West Pier closed 1975 and fell into disrepair. Storms in 2002 and fires in 2003 led to its being deemed beyond repair. Some structured demolition took place 2010 to prepare the way for the i360 observation tower. In 2016 an estimated 4,650,000 people visited the Palace Pier which has gained fame through providing a context for films such as the gangster thriller 'Brighton Rock' and comedy 'Carry On at Your Convenience'.

Exiting the ticket barrier at Brighton station walk straight ahead between the columns bearing blue plaques to David Mocatta

(1806-82) the station architect and John Saxby (18212-1913) pioneer of railway signalling. Continue straight across the forecourt and through the gates past the bus stops down Queen's Road. This commemorates Queen Victoria in whose reign the station arrived (1841). After Queen's Head pub you pass Prince's House with its shields and Imperial House where the BBC is currently located. On the left further down is Sundial House with its elegant tower (1896). Now a Chiropractic Clinic the metal safe door behind the reception desk is a relic of when the building served the National Deposit Bank. The plaque besides the Masonic Centre and Club recalls how 'Freemasons have met in Brighton since 1789'. Brighthelm Church and Community Centre with its garden lies on the junction with Church Road that leads up to the 11th century St Nicholas Church.

As the road levels you pass the fascinating Quadrant Pub before the Clock Tower (1887) commemorating Queen Victoria her Consort Albert, their son Edward Prince of Wales and Alexandra his Princess. Cross North Street continuing your descent to the sea down West Street. In its early days the anglocatholic worship in St Paul's Church (1848) on your right caused 'ritual riots' as the Church of England came to terms with the Oxford Movement. It has fine stained glass windows designed by Pugin. At King's Road you follow the invitation 'Descend subway to beach'. After the toilets turn left and catch the sea air along the Promenade passing Shelter Hall food market, the Fortune of War pub (1882) and the Fishing Museum which has free entry. Head up the slope onto Kings Road heading for the pier clock tower. Turn right onto Brighton Palace Pier walking through or past the Palace of Fun, Palm

Court and Dome Arcade to the dodgems and overhead swinging catapult ride.

Return to Grand Junction Road and cross to Royal Albion Hotel. On this site stood formerly the house of physician Richard Russell (1687-1759) who first promoted the healing power of Brighton's sea water. Turn right and walk around the hotel into Old Steine where fishermen once dried their nets. The Youth Hostel was formerly the Royal York hotel where King Willian IV and Queen Adelaide stayed in 1829. Continue on the pavement, turn left into Castle Square and right before the roundabout into Pavilion Buildings. Head left at India Gate and take the second left turn walking away from the Royal Pavilion to the left of Brighton Dome onto New Road. Turn right and continue past the Unitarian Church to Church Road. Turn left passing Dockerills Ironmongers then cross into Gardner Street in North Laine signed for the station. At the T junction with North Road turn right then left into Kensington Gardens. At the T junction turn right then left along Sydney Street up to Trafalgar Street. Turn left, as signed, up to the station. After passing under the bridge turn right and right again around the railings onto Brighton Station forecourt.

2.6 mile/4.2 km

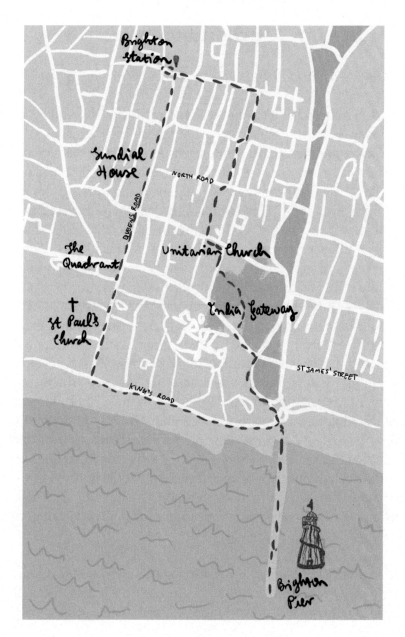

Brighton station

Sundial House

NORTH ROAD

QUEEN'S ROAD

The Quadrant

Unitarian Church

India Gateway

† St Paul's Church

ST JAMES' STREET

KING'S ROAD

Brighton Pier

54

9   Brighton Marina

2.5 mile seaside walk to Brighton Marina returning by bus

In 1806 plans for a harbour were set forth with two stone piers opposite East and West Street joined at their extremities to enclose a harbour space of fourteen acres with docks, a wharf and fifty warehouses. The plans lacked financial support but if this had been forthcoming it would have put pay to the pleasure resort of Brighton & Hove we know today. Pressures continued though well expressed in 1842 by Brighton Brighton brewer George Wigney: 'We are sadly deficient in marine scenery and the means of gratifying a very large proportion of our visitors who are habitually partial to scenes of naval and mercantile activity' (8). By then Southampton had taken from Brighton the cross-Channel steamer trade. In 1855 Southwick Ship Canal at Shoreham Port was opened for shipping aiding the supply of coal to the adjacent gas works (1870) and power station (1907). Brighton visitors found their 'marine scenery' there until momentum gathered to build a Marina to the east of the resort culminating in a successful Town Poll in January 1969. Building took place 1971-9 with ongoing development to this day. Brighton Marina covers approximately 127 acres (0.51 km2) and features a harbour with boatyard and residential housing as well as a variety of leisure and commercial activities that draw visitors as well as walkers heading further east along the Undercliff walk.

From the ticket barrier of Brighton station walk straight ahead between the columns across the forecourt through the gates past the bus stops down Queen's Road to the Clock Tower commemorating Queen Victoria, her successor and their spouses. Cross North Street and continue down to the sea along West Street. At King's Road you follow the invitation 'Descend subway to beach'. After the toilets turn left to proceed along the Esplanade and eventually up the slope onto Kings Road heading past the pier. Continue to the right of the Aquarium onto Madeira Drive and walk along the promenade beside the railings above the beach. Volk's Electric Railway (1883) diagonally opposite the toilets is advertised as 'the world's oldest working electric railway'. You pass the anchor of 'Athina B' beached and refloated 1980 and statue of Brightonian Olympian Steve Ovett, erected 2012 replacing the 1987 original stolen from Preston Park. To your left the Grade 2 listed 865 metre long rusting metal arches are subject of the ongoing Madeira Terrace restoration. Once the eastern boundary of Brighton, Black Rock, named after a large rock below the cliffs now gone, is associated with the Volk's Railway Black Rock terminal. After the station the walk descends an underpass that surfaces at the Marina. Head to the right of the car park along the pavement under the raised road then follow the signed pedestrian way right, under the multi-storey car park, then left. Cross at the crossing continuing in the same direction then turn right to the bus stop to catch a 7, 14B, 47 or 57 bus back to Brighton Station.

2.6 mile/4.2 km

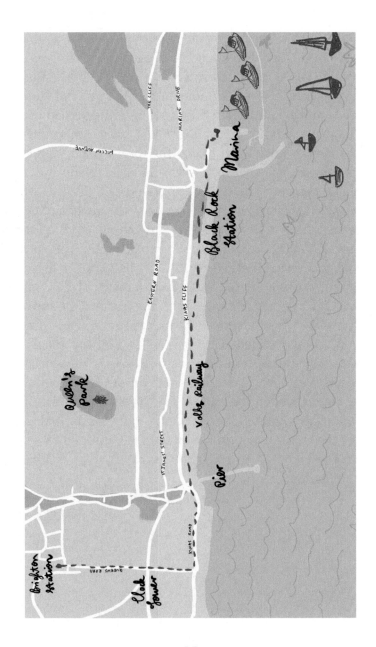

Brighton Station

Clock Tower

Queen's Park

Volks Railway

Pier

Black Rock Station

Marina

QUEENS ROAD

KINGS ROAD

ST JAMES STREET

EASTERN ROAD

KINGS CLIFF

BUCKET AVENUE

THE CLIFF

MARINE DRIVE

10   Preston Manor

3 mile circular walk via Brighton Greenway to Preston Manor returning via Booth Museum

Preston Park is one of the largest green spaces in Brighton & Hove kept green in the driest summer on account of an underground water source. This is the Wellesbourne, Brighton's 'lost river' running below it continuing down to The Level. The lack of a river above ground has been linked to the alleged therapeutic quality of Brighton air. Many coastal resorts have quite damp air as their houses lie alongside rivers heading to sea which soak into their foundations. North of the scenic Park is St Peter's Church and Preston Manor. The redundant Church open to the public was damaged by fire in 1906 and only fragments of its wall paintings survive. The Manor, held once by the Bishop of Chichester, traces back to the 13th century though the present building dates from 1738. 'In 1794 William Stanford bought Preston Manor from his landlord. He leased land to the Prince Regent for a dairy and was paid handsomely when the railway crossed his lands in 1833. He died one of the richest men in Sussex in 1841... In 1905 Ellen and Charles Thomas-Stanford made Preston Manor their main home. Charles was elected Mayor of Brighton in 1910 and Member of Parliament in 1914. The couple died in 1932 but the Stanford legacy lives on at Preston Manor and in the names of roads on the former estate, including Vere Road, Benett Drive, Stanford Avenue and Ellen Street' (9). Said to be 'the most haunted house in Britain' Preston Manor is open to the public and runs as a museum commemorating the Edwardian era and the Stanford family. Exhibitions capturing the everyday life of servants and residents include a fire escape ladder designed for lowering from an upstairs window.

Exiting the ticket barrier at Brighton Station turn left then left again past the cycle storage onto Fleet Street. Continue past the steps to enter Brighton Greenway which follows an old railway track. Descend to New England Road, turn left under the bridge and left down Argyle Road continuing to its junction with Preston Road. Turn left continuing under the viaduct and walk across the pedestrian crossings into Preston Park. Head half right through the Rose Garden to Rotunda Cafe and toilets then left to walk between the tennis courts. Head right then left towards Chalet Cafe and then veer left following the path from which you can access St Peter's Church, Preston Manor and Garden. Re-entering the pavement of Preston Road turn right then left across the pedestrian crossing by the petrol station and walk up South Road. Passing under the railway bridge with the PDSA Pets Hospital to your right, continue left up the steep incline of Millers Road which joins Highcroft Villas at the top. Pause to look back and enjoy the view of the South Downs. Continue to the Dyke Road junction opposite the petrol station. Turn left walking past the Army Reserve Centre barracks opposite Dyke Road Park to the Booth Museum. From there continue along Dyke Road keeping straight ahead at the junction by the Sixth Form College. Turn left before Good Companions Pub down Russell Crescent then right at the junction with Pentonville Road above the railway, pausing to enjoy the view of the Hospital on the horizon. Turn left down Howard Terrace then cross New England Road past The Shakespeare's Head walking up Howard Place. There is a fine view of the railway to your left. Continue onto Terminus Road alongside the large building after which you turn left to arrive back in the forecourt of Brighton Station.

2.8 mile/4.6 km

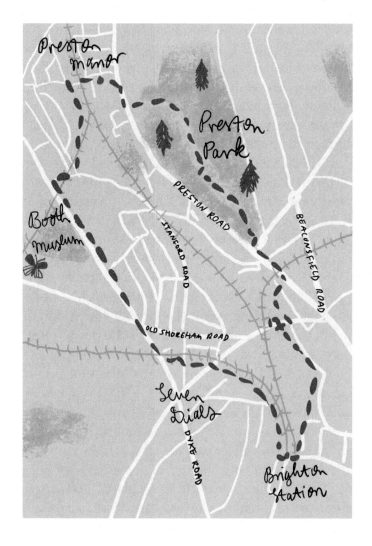

11   Kemp Town

5 mile circular walk via Queen's Park to Kemp Town returning via Madeira Drive

Brighton's diversity fuels its creativity and Kemp Town, built from the 1820s in the wake of the Royal Pavilion, is at the heart of this. Known historically as an actors' and artists' quarter it is closely associated with the gay community of which Brighton & Hove takes special pride. Kemp Town or Kemptown for short came about through the creativity of Thomas Kemp (1782-1844) who 'enjoyed to the full the life of pleasure and sport that was the lot of a fashionable young man in the gay days of the Regent. He was a lavish host and an enthusiastic horseman and excelled in yachting and archery'. Clifford Musgrave notes 'Kemp not only paid for the building of St George's Church out of his own pocket, but he gave to the town the large expanse of open land known as The Level... Despite his enormous wealth, his fortune was entirely absorbed by his various building operations... and he fell into the hands of sharks and usurers... On 10 January 1844 a proclamation of outlawry against Kemp was nailed to the door of St Peter's Church, Brighton while a service was in progress. Four months later he died in Paris in his sixty-first year, and is buried in the cemetery of Père Lachaise' (10).

From the Station forecourt descend the pavement down Queen's Road. Turn left into Gloucester Road continuing across North Laine and a series of pedestrian precincts to the bottom of the road. A path heads left here to join Gloucester Street behind North Laine Brewhouse. Cross Gloucester Place, Valley Gardens and Grand Parade at the pedestrian crossing and ascend Richmond Parade and Place with Brighton Tyre & Exhaust to your right. Continue up the steep steps following the path through the gardens of Grove Hill. At the top cross John Street diagonally right and walk up more steps into Elmore Road. There is another steep ascent here as you turn left then right up into Richmond Street which then descends to its junction with Queens Park Road. Turn left then cross around the old Primitive Methodist Chapel, now a Nursery, down Albion Hill to West Drive. Cross and turn right then left down the sloping path into Queen's Park. Turn right at the bottom continuing with the playground to the left back up to West Drive at the main park entrance. Turn right along Queen's Park Road and immediately left down Upper Park Place enjoying the sea view. Turn left down Mount Pleasant to Edward Street. Cross, walk to the right and turn left down Devonshire Place to St James Street. Cross to view the AIDS memorial in New Steine and turn left to view and maybe visit St Mary's Church. Continue in the same direction along Upper St James's Street crossing Bedford Street into Bristol Road where you can view St John the Baptist Roman Catholic Chapel. Head right at the crossing into St George's Road to St George's Church on the left and the former Sassoon Mausoleum diagonally opposite. At the junction with Eaton Place turn left then right into Chesham Road which becomes Rock Street heading to Eastern Road. Turn right, crossing Sussex Square, then right, following the fine terraced housing on Lewes Crescent down to Marine Parade enjoying the view through the gate of the private gardens. Turn left along Marine Parade, go across the pedestrian crossing, turn right then left down the steps onto Black Rock walking trail. Subject to ongoing development here you can choose a variety of routes and levels heading west along

Madeira Drive or the beach eventually reaching the roundabout at Brighton Pier. Cross to the right of Royal Albion Hotel and continue through or alongside Old Steine Gardens to walk with the Royal Pavilion to your left. Continue through Victoria and Valley Gardens to the left of St Peter's Church into London Road. Turn left up Ann Street past St Bartholomew's Church and School up through the shopping precinct to the pedestrian crossing. Cross Fleet Street and continue up the steps. Head left into Brighton Station.

5.0 mile/8.0 km

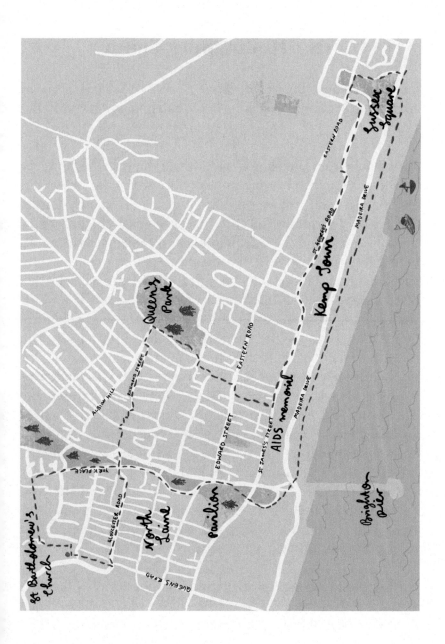

St Bartholomew's church

North Laine

Pavilion

Queen's Park

AIDS memorial

Kemp Town

Sussex Square

Brighton Pier

QUEENS ROAD
GLOUCESTER ROAD
YORK PLACE
ALBION HILL
RICHMOND STREET
EDWARD STREET
EASTERN ROAD
ST JAMES'S STREET
MADEIRA DRIVE
ST GEORGE'S ROAD
EASTERN ROAD
MADEIRA DRIVE

12   Hollingbury Camp

5 mile circular walk via Preston Park and Varndean College to Hollingbury Camp returning via Hollingbury Park and The Level

Just visible from Ditchling Road after crossing the A27 towards Brighton & Hove, on a promontory forward to the left within Hollingbury golf course, is Brighton's little known Castle. 'Hollingbury Castle or hill fort... is to the east of Hollingbury housing estate and the Ditchling Road. Although considered to be Iron Age (450-250 BC), the mounding of four round barrows suggests even Bronze Age (3300-1200 BC) people held this place sacred. Now all that remains are thickets of gorse which shine yellow in spring and are home to linnets and goldfinch' (11). On a visit to the site the ditch is evident from which chalk diggings would have been thrown up to make the rampart inside. This would have been strengthened with wooden beams to dispel invaders. The camp (castle) defenders patrolled the square rampart walkway a mile and a quarter (2km) in length enclosing 9 acres (3.6 hectares). There is documentary evidence suggesting the ancient fort served as site of a beacon from the middle ages onwards. Since 1908 the fort has been situated within Hollingbury Park Golf Course. It is adjacent to Wild Park, Brighton & Hove's largest nature reserve with woodland walks and views over the city and beyond. On a clear day you can see the Isle of Wight 45 miles away.

Exiting the ticket barrier at Brighton Station turn left then left again past the cycle storage and taxi rank onto Stroudley Road. Continue past the steps to enter Brighton Greenway which follows an old railway track. Descend to New England Road, turn left under the bridge and left down Argyle Road continuing to its junction with Preston Road. Turn left continuing under the viaduct and walk across the pedestrian crossings into Preston Park. Join the path to the right of the Rose Garden and Rotunda Cafe. Continue straight ahead keeping to the right of the Table Tennis Table and Play Park. After the Clock Tower head half right towards the car park and at the cricket ground enter the path between the hedges leading to Preston Park Gate. Continue in the same direction traversing Preston Drove on the zebra crossing past St Mary's Catholic Church along Surrenden Road. After Harrington Road cross to join the path on the wooded island in the centre of the dual carriageway. Continue right along this island at the junction with Surrenden Crescent. You keep Varndean College fields on your right. Take a right turn to continue along Surrenden Road around the perimeter of the College fields. At the T junction cross Ditchling Road and continue left along the pavement passing the phone mast and reservoir. Turn right into the access road for Hollingbury Golf Course.

Take the second permissive footpath to the left, the one just before the car park, and bear right heading for the Golf Course. When the path passes to the left between the hedges the flat remains of the hill fort come into view. Continue straight ahead up across the Golf Course and at the top of the hill follow the permissive footpath sign right to enter Hollingbury Camp. Walk left along the perimeter bank to the trig point enjoying views of the South Downs. Continue around the roughly square sided fort where you catch sight of Falmer Stadium (2008). At the footpath junction turn left then left again along the hedge. Turn

68

right at the footpath sign and proceed around the golf tee. At the path crossing with the display board turn right and continue as the path bends to and fro before reaching the T at the break in the hedge. Take a detour left to view the Dewpond more closely then head back to follow the path with a sea view along the hedge to the right of the large field.

Proceed on your descent through the car park and then to the left of the football pitch and playground of Hollingdean Park. At Lynchet Close turn right and at the Community Centre take a left turn onto Brentwood Road. Turn right at the junction descending Stephens Road to The Crossway. Turn left then right down Horton Road enjoying the sea view ahead. At the T junction turn right onto Davey Drive then left on reaching Upper Hollingdean Road. Take the first right cutting onto Hollingdean Lane. Turn right to walk beside Hollingdean's immense Material Recovery Facility and Waste Transfer Station with its signal dragonflies bearing left up onto Ditchling Road. Take a left turn and continue down to The Level with St Peter's Church on the horizon. Turn right at the Bat & Ball pub to walk along Oxford Street to London Road. Cross and enter Ann Street. Continue past St Bartholomew's Church and School up the stairs back to Brighton Station.

5.2 mile/8.3 km

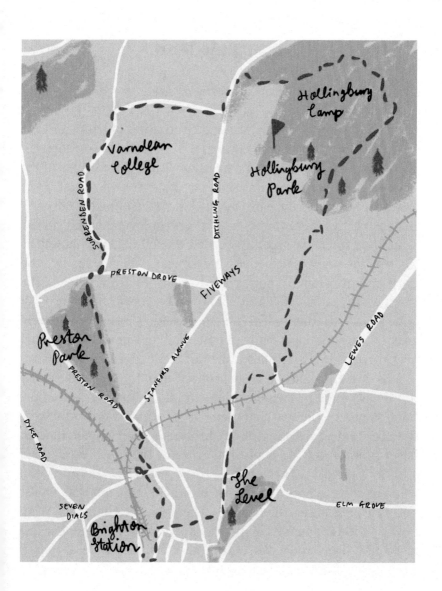

13   Saltdean

6 mile walk via Undercliff Walk to Saltdean returning by bus

The ongoing part national funded restoration of Saltdean Lido (1938) echoes its origin and that of the Undercliff Walk almost a century ago. Clifford Musgrave writes: 'After the collapse of the General Strike (1926)... unemployment continued to rise... the great depression of the early 1930s descended upon the country. A constructive attempt to relieve unemployment and at the same time to create urgently needed coastal defences as well as to provide new attractive amenities was made by the Corporation when a new coastal road to Rottingdean, the Marine Drive, was made at a cost of £180,000 between 1929 and 1932, together with the construction of new concrete groynes and a sea wall with an under cliff promenade stretching over three miles from Black Rock to Rottingdean and Saltdean, at a cost of £400,000. A large proportion of the cost was met by the Government's Unemployment Grant Committee, and in the final stages of the work as many as 500 men were employed, some of them consisting of Brighton unemployed, and at least half coming from the depressed areas of the north of England and South Wales. The miners proved especially skilful at the work of cutting back the face of the chalk cliffs to a safe angle, and in constructing the new sea defences. The Undercliff Walk now provides an agreeable promenade not only in summer but in winter, when one can enjoy the sunshine while sheltered from the cold north and east winds' (12).

From the ticket barrier at Brighton Station walk straight ahead between the columns across the forecourt through the gates past the bus stops down Queen's Road to the Clock Tower. Continue down to the sea along West Street. At King's Road you follow the invitation 'Descend subway to beach'. After the toilets turn left to proceed along the Esplanade and eventually up the slope onto Kings Road heading past the pier. Continue to the right of the Aquarium onto Madeira Drive and walk along the promenade beside the railings above the beach. Once the eastern boundary of Brighton, Black Rock, named after a large rock below the cliffs now gone, is associated with the electric railway's Black Rock terminal. After the terminal continue straight ahead up the slope keeping to the right beside the cycle track on the pavement by the fence.

Descend the slope which joins the Undercliff Walk signed England Coast Path and pass through the metal gates. Walk to the left of the ASDA supermarket with the cliffs on your left. This cliff section is covered with wire netting to protect walkers below from loose stones. On the right a yacht basin appears where boats are moored accessible to residents of Brighton Marina apartments across the water. After the pool the boatyard makes interesting viewing and can be more fully accessed on a promenade off to the right beside the wall which marks the end of the Marina. Beach stones on the path give evidence of how the sea makes its mark despite the walls. Look back at the Marina noting the 'dolosse' or reinforced concrete blocks alongside its walls. These are found on the Undercliff Walk at times reinforcing sets of groynes in tempering the waves. Ovingdean beach has stairs up to the village, toilets, beach huts and a cafe. At Rottingdean beach you pass under the Quarterdeck Promontory to a larger cafe with toilets and the hard path continues to the east of Saltdean. Retrace your steps to ascend the slope or pass through the tunnel under White Cliffs Cafe (1933-4) and up steps to the bus stop opposite Saltdean Lido. Catch a 12, 12a, 12x, 13x, 14, 14b, 14c, 27 or 27b bus back to Brighton Station.

5.8 mile/9.3 km

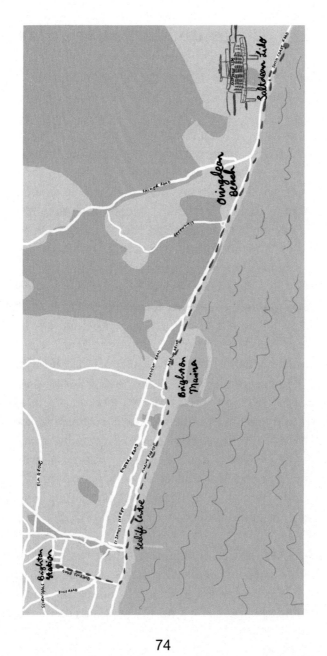

14   Brighton Marina circular

6 mile circular walk via seaside to Brighton Marina returning via Kemp Town

Brighton expanded from a fishing community to a resort fuelled by royalty. Its eastward expansion linked to the Prince Regent's conversion of a farmhouse into his Pavilion. 'The Prince's example attracted ambitious and distinguished schemes for development... Royal Crescent... exceptional not only for its graceful alignment but for the fact that it is faced not with brick but with tiles. Marine Parade... on which it stands... consists of private residences of architectural distinction added at later dates in the Regency period... the most spacious of town-planning schemes...called Kemp Town' (13). As the resort developed fuller access to the sea was provided by three piers one of which survives and from 1971-9 the Marina, destination of this walk, which passes the site of the old Chain Pier (1823-1896) level with New Steine and returns through the splendours of Kemp Town. These include Proud Cabaret, formerly the mausoleum built 1892 by Sir Albert Sassoon in the oriental style of the Royal Pavilion. A striking but more sombre feature is the UK's only dedicated AIDS memorial at the top of New Steine. Romany Mark Bruce's cast bronze figures, one male and one androgynous, soar heavenwards forming a shadow in the shape of the red ribbon symbol for HIV/AIDS awareness.

From the ticket barrier of Brighton station walk straight ahead between the columns across the forecourt through the gates past the bus stops down Queen's Road to the Clock Tower commemorating Queen Victoria, her successor and their spouses. Cross North Street and continue down to the sea along West Street. At King's Road you follow the invitation 'Descend subway to beach'. After the toilets turn left to proceed along the Esplanade and eventually up the slope onto Kings Road heading past the pier. Continue to the right of the Aquarium onto Madeira Drive and walk along the promenade beside the railings above the beach. Volk's Electric Railway (1883) diagonally opposite the toilets is advertised as 'the world's oldest working electric railway'. You pass the anchor of 'Athina B' beached and refloated 1980 and statue of Brightonian Olympian Steve Ovett, erected 2012 replacing the 1987 original stolen from Preston Park. To your left the Grade 2 listed 865 metre long rusting metal arches are subject of the ongoing Madeira Terrace restoration. Once the eastern boundary of Brighton, Black Rock, named after a large rock below the cliffs now gone, is associated with the Volk's Railway Black Rock terminal. After the station the walk descends an underpass that surfaces at the Marina. Head to the right of the car park along the pavement under the raised road then follow the signed pedestrian way right, under the multi-storey car park to the cinema and restaurants. Head left and across the road to enter either the promenade to the right or the north wall promenade straight ahead. This leads to the sea wall where you can walk left to the Under Cliff Walk or right to the end of the harbour viewing harboured boats and sea traffic.

Head out of the Marina towards the Under Cliff Walk but turn left under the road, walk up through the garden path and up the steps to King's Cliff. Turn right, cross Marine Parade at the pedestrian crossing and head left then right into Lewes Crescent leading to Sussex Square. Enjoy the views of the gardens, which are private, as you ascend the terrace of fine Regency houses. Turn left along Eastern Road then left down Rock Street continuing along Chesham Road. Cross Eaton Place into St George's Road. Proud Cabaret, the former Sassoon Mausoleum is on the corner of Paston Place diagonally opposite St. George's Church. Follow St. George's Road then Bristol Road past St. John the Baptist Roman Catholic Chapel once frequented by Maria Fitzherbert, controversial consort of George IV when Prince Regent. Brighton Flea Market is a possible detour. Continue to St Mary's Church and across into St James Street, passing the AIDS memorial in New Steine on the left. At Old Steine cross the pedestrian crossing to walk in front of Brighton War Memorial crossing again into Castle Square. Continue straight ahead, noting the India Gate and Royal Pavilion to the right, into North Street past the Chapel Royal and up to the Clock Tower. Turn right into Queen's Road and walk up to Brighton Station.

5.8 mile/9.3 km

15   Devil's Dyke

6 mile walk via Monarch's Way to Devil's Dyke returning by bus

The deep sharp cut out from the smooth slope of the Downs five miles above Brighton & Hove is a puzzle. Devil's Dyke is water worn but closed at each end. No wonder theories of an external impact developed. An interrupted work of the Devil seeking to channel the sea over Christian Sussex is the legend behind the name. This intriguing ravine at the high point of the South Downs, once crowned by an ancient hill camp, has always drawn visitors not least in Victorian times. A railway zig-zagging up to Devil's Dyke was opened 1887 and an aerial cableway across the 1,000 foot (305 meter) ravine 1894. The Dyke Steep Grade Railway (1897-1909) carried over 275,000 passengers a year as well as farm produce and supplies for the hotel. The aerial cableway and steam railway were a great draw but became less so with the arrival of the motor car when visitors could make their own way to the hotel and its scenic viewpoint. Brighton entrepreneur Leslie Kramer attempted to rebuild trade at the hotel after the Second World War through a number of attractions. His proposal in 1964 to build a one-fifth scale replica of Egypt's Abu Simbel Temple into the side of the Dyke was rejected (14).

From the ticket barrier continue straight ahead to the station forecourt and turn right. Cross the pedestrian crossing and turn right on the pavement up Terminus Road crossing before West Hill Tavern onto Howard Place enjoying views to the right across Brighton. Brick built St Luke, Prestonville (1875) is on the horizon straight ahead. At Shakespeare's Head pub, cross Chatham Place continuing up Howard Terrace to Pentonville Road. Turn right enjoying the view from the bridge of the railway line to Hove then cross left into Russell Crescent walking to Good Companions pub on the junction. Turn right along Dyke Road and left across the pedestrian crossing at the junction with Old Shoreham Road (A270) by the Sixth Form College.

Continue left along Old Shoreham Road on the pavement at the junction and cross the zebra crossing to walk alongside the playing fields which are accessible out of school hours. After crossing Shirley Drive enter Hove Recreation Ground by the cafe and continue in the same direction on the path between the trees which exits onto the main road. Take a right turn immediately into the signed bridleway. Keep left at the path junction and continue to Goldstone Crescent. Cross into Monarch's Way which heads diagonally across family friendly Hove Park behind. Turn right at the climbing boulders and left before the miniature railway exiting the park up The Droveway past British Engineerium to Nevill Road. Brighton & Hove Greyhound Stadium is to the left just off this road. Cross Woodland Drive and ascend Nevill Road. Cross the zebra crossing to enter Court Farm Road passing St George's Roman Catholic Church. Before St Peter's Church, divert left down Holmes Avenue to view West Blatchington Windmill (c1820).

Return to Court Farm Road, turn left past St Peter's and cross Hangleton Road at the crossing into Clarke Avenue. Take the first right into Downland Drive which bends left to follow wooded access land. As the Drive bends left at the top head right into the signed pathway through the trees. After the sports ground the path descends to a T junction. Head right to cross the A27 over the footbridge. Continue straight ahead onto the metalled path which lies on an abandoned railway track and continue past West Hove Golf Course on your left. Just before Brighton & Hove Golf Clubhouse head left at the path junction and continue on the tarmac bridleway to Devil's Dyke Road. Cross the road and head left along the stone chip path to the road junction. Head across the road in the same direction onto a narrower path which runs parallel to the road up to Devil's Dyke Inn. Take time to enjoy the views of Sussex and the sea before catching the bus back to Brighton Station which runs at weekends and on bank holidays.

5.9 mile/9.5 km

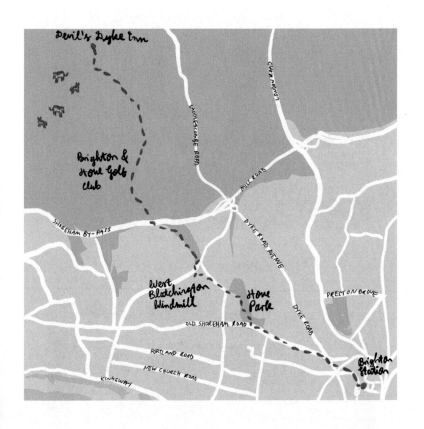

AIDS memorial in Kemptown

Brighton Alquds Mosque on Dyke Road

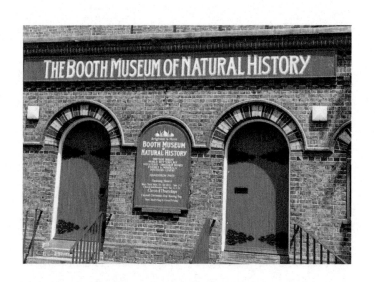

Booth Museum of Natural History

Sassoon Mausoleum, now a Kemptown club

Anchor of Athina B beached in 1980

Drove Road Stud above Woodingdean

West Blatchington Windmill

Circus pony in Brighton Cemetery

Chattri Memorial

St Bartholomew's Church interior

Jenny Lind train model on Brighton Greenway

Neoclassical Royal Spa Nursery at Queen's Park

Battle of Trafalgar Pub above Brighton Station

Sussex County Cricket Club

Sundial House on Queen's Road

Dragonflies at Hollingdean Material Recovery Facility

British Engineerium museum in Hove

Jaipur Gate (1886) outside Hove Museum

Preston Park Clock Tower

Jonathan Wright's Constellation (2018) on Hove Plinth

16   Stanmer House

6 mile walk via Patcham to Stanmer House and Falmer returning by train

Stanmer Park was laid out by the Chichester family who in 1713 acquired the land and commissioned the architect Nicholas Dubois to build Stanmer House incorporating the remains of an earlier building. The House, built in Palladian style, is adjacent to Stanmer Church, also rebuilt by the Earl of Chichester in the nineteenth century. During the Second World War local residents were evacuated after the Stanmer Estate was commandeered by the military for training. Damage was done to the House during artillery practice. After the First World War three Earls of Chichester died in short succession causing prohibitive death duties and the estate had to be sold. In 1947 Brighton Corporation made the far reaching decision to purchase the fine Georgian House and its estate including the villages of Stanmer and Falmer. This decision facilitated provision of sites for new schools, a College of Education and the University of Sussex which received its Royal Charter 1961. These educational institutes lie conveniently south of Stanmer Park, with its recreational facilities and proximity to the South Downs, alongside the A27 and railway which serve easy access to them from Brighton & Hove and also to Falmer football stadium.

Exiting the ticket barrier at Brighton Station turn left then left again past the cycle storage and taxi rank onto Stroudley Road. Continue past the steps to enter Brighton Greenway which follows an old railway track. Descend to New England Road, turn left under the bridge and left down Argyle Road continuing to its junction with Preston Road. Turn left continuing under the viaduct and walk across the pedestrian crossings into Preston Park. Join the path to the right of the Rose Garden and Rotunda Cafe. Continue straight ahead keeping to the right of the Table Tennis Table and Play Park. After the Clock Tower head half right towards the car park and at the cricket ground enter the path between the hedges leading to Preston Park Gate.

Continue in the same direction crossing Preston Drove on the zebra crossing past St Mary's Catholic Church along Surrenden Road. After Harrington Road cross to join the path on the wooded island in the centre of the dual carriageway. Continue right along this island at the junction with Surrenden Crescent. You keep Varndean College fields on your right. After the second junction with Surrenden Crescent the island disappears. Take the left hand pavement as the long gentle incline continues. The road merges with Braybon Avenue at the top where you can enjoy scenic views of the Downs ahead. After Brighton Elim Church Fountain Centre (formerly Christ the King Anglican Church) and St Thomas More Church continue straight ahead along Warmdene Road past Patcham High School.

Cross Ladies Mile Road into Ladies Mile Close and then turn right up the grassy incline besides the hedge and fence. At the white railings continue into the copse then head down at the junction to walk behind the houses of Mackie Avenue. Head left at the junction with the tree in the middle and continue in the same direction across the tarmac path with steps to the left. Pass through the wooden gate up the slope heading left through

94

Ladies Mile Nature Reserve up to another wooden gate. Turn left then pass through the pedestrian gate at the left of the large gate and continue straight ahead past the transmitter. Take a break at the ample seat by the gate to look back over Brighton. Head through the gate and hedge onto the pavement beside the roundabout. Turn left then carefully cross past the Worthing sign to the grass island and pavement which leads across the bridge over the A27. At the second roundabout cross by the No Entry signs onto the pavement heading right then left through the hedge.

Turn right along the footpath which leads up to a gate. Continue through the gate across the field to the gate on Ditchling Road. Cross with care diagonally left into the signed Public Bridleway and continue across the front of the car park onto the metalled road. At the footpath junction continue as signed down the same road to Stanmer Village. At the crossroads turn right walking past the cottages and Stanmer Tea Rooms to Stanmer Church with the pond to its left. At the T junction turn right then left through the Churchyard to seats where you can view Stanmer House. Walk across to the left of the House and join the footpath which heads left through Stanmer Park. At the cafeteria head left then right to the old gate houses. Turn left along the pavement then half right onto the footpath shared with cyclists. Head right at the end and pass through the subway then right up to the steps ascending to Falmer railway station.

6.1 mile/9.8 km

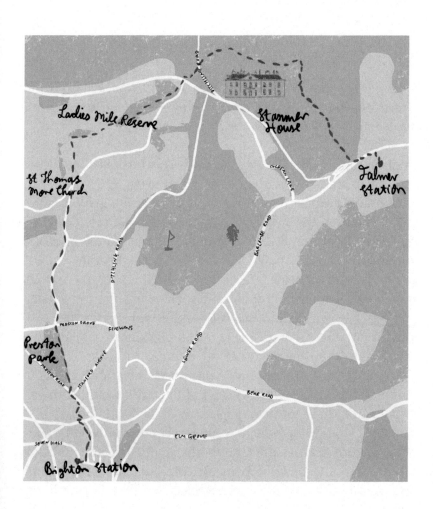

Ladies Mile Reserve

Stanmer House

St Thomas More Church

Falmer Station

COLDEAN LANE

BRACILINE ROAD

DITCHLING ROAD

PRESTON GROVE

FIVEWAYS

Preston Park

STANFORD AVENUE

LOWES ROAD

PRESTON ROAD

BEAR ROAD

ELM GROVE

SEVEN DIALS

Brighton station

17   Hove Lagoon

6.5 mile circular walk via Sussex County Cricket Club and Hove Museum to Hove Lagoon returning along the seafront via Brunswick Square and the Peace Statue

Brighton and Hove Borough Council was formed 1997 after a poll of residents weighed the advantages of one tier of government heavier than Hove's fear of domination by Brighton and inclination towards Sussex as a whole. The vote paved the way for Brighton & Hove attaining city status in 2000. 'Although the city now operates as a single entity, locals generally still consider Brighton and Hove to be separate settlements with different identities. Hove is largely residential and has its own distinct seafront and established town centre located around George Street, while Brighton has a higher profile as the country's most popular seaside resort, a significant digital economy, and hosts several festivals of national prominence. Recognition of the city's twin identities is evident from the continued popularity of the local saying "Hove, actually", a phrase which long predates unification. Some organisations such as the local football club, Brighton and Hove Albion, and the bus company Brighton & Hove, predate the unification of the towns by several decades' (15). This walk cuts diagonally across the city to the Lagoon passing some of the sights of Hove.

Exit the ticket barrier at Brighton Station and turn right, cross the pedestrian crossing and head right along the pavement up Terminus Road. The hill you are climbing was partly removed to build the immense station terminus on your right. Follow the road to Brighton's remarkable Seven Dials junction and continue in the same direction along Goldsmid then Davigdor Road. The walk passes St Mary & St Abraam Coptic Church (formerly St Thomas Anglican Church) on the left and The Palmeira pub on your right before heading left down Palmeira Avenue. Turn right at Brighton & Hove Reform Synagogue (1966) onto Eaton Road and take a detour right for Sussex County Cricket Club. Continue across the front of the ticket office turning right at the end of the white buildings to access Sussex Cricket Museum, open on match days, and a view across the cricket ground famed also as a concert venue.

Return to Eaton Road heading to All Saints, Hove, the spacious interior of which can be viewed through glass security doors. Turn left down The Drive and right along Church Road passing Hove Town Hall and St Andrew's Church into New Church Road. Continue to the Jaipur Gate in the garden of Hove Museum & Art Gallery. Commissioned in 1886 for the Colonial and Indian Exhibition in South Kensington it was donated to the museum in 1926. The gate has inscriptions in English, Sanskrit and Latin. These applaud both the British empire and the east through puns: 'ubi virtus ibi victoria' (where virtue lies so does victory/Victoria) and 'ex oriente lux' (light comes from the east/East). The museum has free admission but is closed Tuesday and Wednesday. Continue along New Church Road to Aldrington House which served as Lady Chichester Hospital (1920), a pioneering hospital for the treatment of nervous disorders in women and children. Head left down Westbourne Villas crossing Kingsway via the traffic islands onto a path to the left of a croquet lawn. Turn left to walk right around Hove & Kingsway Bowling Club onto the Western Esplanade continuing past toilets to decorated covered seats where the walk heads right down the steps to Hove Lagoon.

Walk right round the elliptical Lagoon which returns you to the Promenade heading east past the beach huts in front of Hove Lawns and the sculpture on Hove Plinth (2018). Take a detour into the Georgian terraces of Brunswick Square and maybe visit the heritage centre Regency Town House (no 13). Continue along the Promenade past the Peace Statue (1912) on the border between Hove and Brighton and British Airways i360 tower (2016) to Brighton Centre (1977). Turn left to walk up West Street to the Clock Tower continuing up Queen's Road back to Brighton Station.

6.4 mile/10.3 km

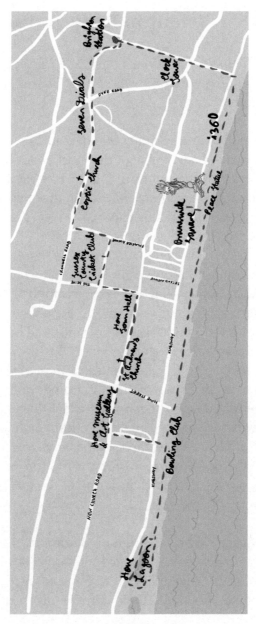

18   Brighton Racecourse

7 mile circular walk via Queen's Park and the Nature Reserve to Brighton Racecourse returning via East Brighton Golf Course and Kemptown

'The race-ground is exceedingly well adapted to the purpose for which it is intended and is one of the most beautifully situated spots in the world' was a comment made by a Brighton visitor of 1789. 'It is situated on Whitehawk Hill, on the edge of the South Downs, about four hundred feet above sea level and a mile from the coast. The geology of the downs is Upper Chalk; therefore the going is nearly always good. The track has the form of a horseshoe one-and-a-half miles in length. This makes it one of the few British courses not to form a complete circuit.. The Duke of Cumberland organised the first public racing at the current site in 1783... Early races were contested by members of the armed forces who were garrisoned in the town... According to legend, King George IV, when still Prince of Wales, invented hurdle racing at Brighton while out riding with aristocratic friends. They found some sheep pens which they proceeded to jump.... Crowds rose to over 20,000 in the period following the Second World War. At the time, grandstands existed on both sides of the home straight... Today, Brighton is one of the smaller racecourses in Britain in terms of the quality of racing and prize money offered' (16).

Exiting the ticket barrier at Brighton Station turn left then left again past the cycle storage and taxi rank onto Stroudley Road. Descend the stairs and cross New England Street into Ann Street down to London Road. Cross into Oxford Street continuing from the Bat & Ball pub across Ditchling Road into The Level heading past the public toilets and Water Feature to the pedestrian crossing. Cross the A270 turn left then right for a steep ascent up Southover Street into Hanover passing Phoenix Halls on your right, Annunciation Church on your left just down Washington Street and the Community Centre. At the mini roundabout turn half right up Montreal Road. Turn left down Albion Hill continuing across Queens Park Road to Queen's Park. Turn right then left down the slope. Turn left walking on the lower path beside the railings. Continue to the metal gate. Divert left to view the Park Monument. Head through the gate up the path to the left of the Clock Tower past the Quiet Garden to East Drive and directly across into Evelyn Terrace.

Take a left turn along Freshfield Road. Cross the road at the island crossing and in a short distance take a right turn down Dawson Terrace. At the T cross diagonally right into the signed footpath. As you enter the Nature Reserve woodland continue straight on up the steep stepped path. At the junction with the wide path turn left. Pause at the seat named Tom's Place to enjoy the view across Brighton. Before the loving-gate head right up the slope towards the TV Station. Take a rest on the seat to enjoy the sea view. Continue left through the gate then immediately right up to the footpath on the right side of the racecourse. Turn left heading for the Grandstand, cross the road and proceed on the footpath which continues to the right of the track. Cross the main road at the top of the racecourse onto the signed bridleway which continues to a junction where you can cross the racecourse. Detour to the bus stop by the car park at the top of the racecourse if you want to shorten the walk otherwise continue down to the right of the 'gallop' descent with scenic coastal views. St Dunstans Blind Veteran Centre and Roedean School are on the horizon to the left.

After the racecourse the footpath follows East Brighton Golf Club course up and then down past the Club House (open to walkers for refreshment) descending the Club access road to Roedean Road. Continue across Wilson Avenue opposite the skeletal Gasometer. Cross Whitehawk Road and then left over Bristol Gardens to walk past the shops and LIDL supermarket. Turn right along Eastern Road then left down Rock Street continuing along Chesham Road. Cross Eaton Place into St George's Road. The former Sassoon Mausoleum is on the corner of Paston Place diagonally opposite St. George's Church. Follow St. George's Road past St. John the Baptist Roman Catholic Chapel once frequented by Maria Fitzherbert, controversial consort of George IV when Prince Regent. Brighton Flea Market is a possible detour. Continue to St Mary's Church and across into St James Street, passing the AIDS memorial in New Steine on the left. At Old Steine cross the pedestrian crossing to walk in front of Brighton War Memorial crossing again into Castle Square. Continue straight ahead, noting the India Gate and Royal Pavilion to the right, into North Street walking up to the Clock Tower. Turn right into Queen's Road and walk up to Brighton Station.

7.0 mile/11.2 km

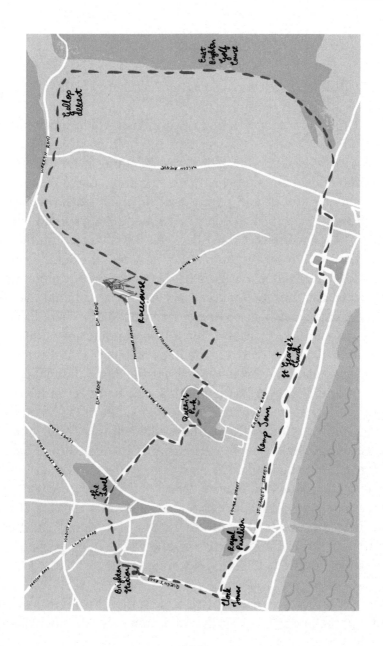

East Brighton Golf Course

Gallop descent

WARREN ROAD

WATSON AVENUE

MANOR HILL

Racecourse

ELM GROVE

ELM GROVE

FRANCHIE AVENUE

FRESHFIELD ROAD

QUEEN'S PARK ROAD

Queen's Park

St George's Church

EASTERN ROAD

Kemp Town

(LEWES) ROAD

UPPER LEWES ROAD

The Level

EDWARD STREET

VIADUCT ROAD

LONDON ROAD

ST JAMES'S STREET

PRESTON ROAD

Royal Pavilion

Brighton Station

QUEEN'S ROAD

Clock Tower

19   Lewes

8 mile walk to Lewes via Jugg's Road returning by train

Once Brighton was most famous for its fish which supplied the county town of Lewes. The ancient Jugg's Road is named after the juggs or baskets full of fish carried along it for centuries. Brighton is first mentioned as 'Bristemestune' in the Domesday Book valued at £12 and paying rent of 4,000 herrings. These would be carried to the county town along Jugg's Road which remains the most direct route between the two communities on foot. This walk from Brighton to Lewes across the South Downs follows Drove Avenue, recalling the history of driving animals to and from pasture or to market in Lewes, a traditional market town. Archaeologists trace Anglo Saxon habitation here back to the sixth century. In 1066 William the Conqueror granted his retainer William de Warenne the Rape of Lewes, land stretching along the Ouse valley from the coast to the Surrey boundary. De Warenne built Lewes Castle and his wife founded the Cluniac Priory of St Pancras around 1081. Other sights of Lewes include a 16th-century timber-framed house known as Anne of Cleves House. Anne's husband King Henry VIII instigated the English Reformation which included seizure by the crown of Lewes Priory. His daughter Queen Mary I (1553-8) reversed her father's action so that in her reign Lewes was the site of the burning at the stake of seventeen Protestant martyrs. Commemorating these martyrs is one of the main purposes of the Lewes Bonfire held each 5 November (17).

Exiting the ticket barrier at Brighton Station turn left then left again past the cycle storage and taxi rank onto Stroudley Road.

Descend the stairs and cross New England Street into Ann Street down to London Road. Cross into Oxford Street continuing across Ditchling Road into The Level heading diagonally left at the public toilets to the north-east corner of the park. Cross Union Road and go straight ahead along Lewes Road past St Martin's Church. Cross the road and enter the Cemetery just before The Gladstone Pub. On Sundays the cemetery opens later at 11am. Continue towards Woodvale Crematorium following the road left up to Bear Road. Cross the road and turn right to walk up beside the City Cemetery walls. When you reach the top of Bear Road take the farm track to the left parallel to Warren Road which continues above Brighton Racecourse. After this becomes a cycle track, keep right at the junction and continue north of Woodingdean.

Cross Falmer Road with care into Drove Avenue to walk across the South Downs. At the junction after the telecommunications mast on Newmarket Hill keep right after which you enter the ancient Jugg's Road (track). After a short distance South Downs Way joins this track from the left. Continue along Jugg's Road at the junction when South Downs Way parts company to head right. The track skirts Kingston descending into Lewes across the A27 and the railway. At the end of Jugg's Road continue straight ahead at the road junction to enter Southover High Street passing Anne of Cleves House. After the right hand junction to Lewes Priory ruins the walk turns left down to the railway station for trains back to Brighton.

7.9 mile/12.7 km

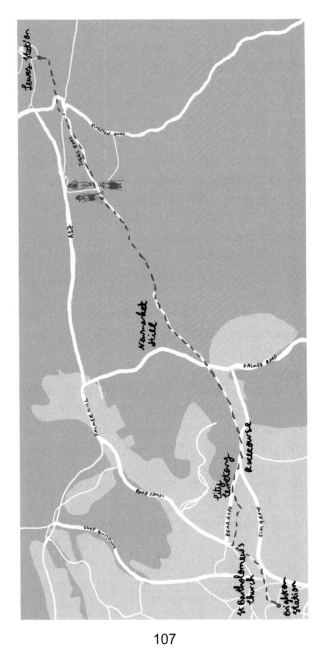

20   Jack & Jill

8 mile walk via Preston Park and Patcham to Jack & Jill windmills returning from Hassocks Station

Brighton & Hove are protected from cold north winds by the Downs. Clayton's windmills atop the South Down have exploited the same winds. Jill was built in 1852, Jack in 1865. Though their working life ended over a century ago, thanks to Mid Sussex District Council Jill is still in working order, open to the public most Sundays between May and September, producing flour on an occasional basis. This walk up to the windmills passes some of the sights of north Brighton starting with Preston Park and heading north through Patcham and up the Downs past the domed Chattri memorial commemorating Indian soldiers who died whilst being cared for at the Royal Pavilion 1914-5. There are splendid views of Brighton & Hove looking back on arrival at the South Downs Way and across Mid Sussex from the other side of the windmills.

Exiting the ticket barrier at Brighton Station turn left then left again past the cycle storage and taxi rank onto Stroudley Road. Continue past the steps to enter Brighton Greenway which follows an old railway track. Descend to New England Road, turn left under the bridge and left down Argyle Road continuing to its junction with Preston Road. Turn left continuing under the viaduct and walk across the pedestrian crossings into Preston Park. Join the path to the right of the Rose Garden and Rotunda Cafe. Continue straight ahead keeping to the right of the Table Tennis Table and Play Park. After the Clock Tower head half right towards the car park and at the cricket ground enter the path between the hedges leading to Preston Park Gate. Continue in the same direction crossing Preston Drove on the zebra crossing past St Mary's Catholic Church along Surrenden Road. After Harrington Road cross to join the path on the wooded island in the centre of the dual carriageway. Continue right along this island at the junction with Surrenden Crescent. You keep Varndean College fields on your right. After the second junction with Surrenden Crescent the island disappears.

Take the left hand pavement as the long gentle incline continues. The road merges with Braybon Avenue at the top where you can enjoy scenic views of the Downs ahead. Continue along and then down Braybon Avenue. After Brighton Elim Church Fountain Centre (formerly Christ the King Anglican Church) and St Thomas More Church turn left along Carden Avenue. Turn right at the shops proceeding along Patchdean with Patcham High School on the right to the Clock Tower where the walk proceeds half left up Vale Avenue. At the top of the hill you can take a left detour down Church Hill to visit All Saints, Patcham which has stood on this hill for 1000 years. Cross Vale Road opposite Patcham Court Farmhouse and continue on the footpath to just beyond the traffic island. Cross and head in the same direction across the road bridge. Continue across the A27 slip road, turn left and walk to the right up the road then left onto the Sussex Border Path (SBP) heading up onto the South Downs.

Take a right detour off SBP to visit the Chattri memorial. After this you pass a copse on your left and continue through a large gate. Take a left turn along the Bridleway leaving SBP. Continue through a small gate, turn right alongside a hedged fence then left following the footpath away from the hedge. After a short distance take the signed right hand path which leads along the perimeter of Pyecombe Golf Course. After New Barn Farm this path joins the South Downs Way (SDW). Enjoy the view back over Brighton & Hove. At the path junction the walk leaves SDW proceeding left to the windmills Jack and then Jill.

Turn right to walk through the car park with its splendid views of Sussex. Go through the gate and descend the field on the Bridleway parallel to the fence on the left. Continue left on this path which descends to a signed junction. Go left through the adjacent gate continuing down to the road. Turn left along the road past the Church of St John the Baptist, Clayton where you can make a detour to view the medieval wall paintings. At the A273 turn right and cross with care at the top of the B2112. At this point a detour across the road is possible to view the turreted and castellated portal of Clayton Tunnel and maybe visit the adjacent Jack & Jill Pub. Otherwise continue right along the footpath which follows to the right of the railway line into Hassocks. Cross Keymer Road then turn left along the footpath to pass under the railway bridge. Ascend stairs to the right and continue into Hassocks Station to catch a train back to Brighton.

8.2 mile/13.2 km

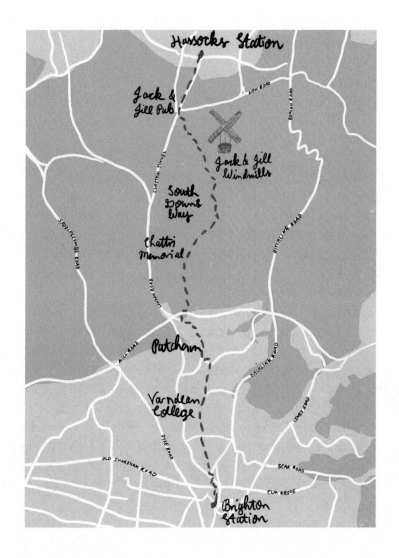

Hassocks Station

Jack &
Jill Pub

NEW ROAD

BEACON ROAD

Jack & Jill
Windmills

CLAYTON TUNNEL

South
Downs
Way

SADDLESCOMBE ROAD

DITCHLING ROAD

Chattri
Memorial

Patcham

MILL ROAD

LONDON ROAD

DITCHLING ROAD

Varndean
College

LEWES ROAD

DYKE ROAD

OLD SHOREHAM ROAD

BEAR ROAD

ELM GROVE

Brighton
Station

21   Southease

8.5 mile walk via Woodingdean and South Downs Way to Southease returning by train

O green, translucent Downs! Soft-shadowed, lifted high! What magic fills you, that you stand, untouched by Time's relentless hand, as God first breathed you on the morning sky? Ruth Wainwright's poem Enchantment (18)

Easy access to the South Downs Way (SDW) is a benefit of living in Brighton & Hove. A range of chalk hills running from Winchester to Eastbourne the Downs are dry underfoot in all seasons and not very high which, with the well signed SDW, helps accessibility for all ages. This walk is to Southease, on SDW just south of Lewes, a major portal to these hills for visitors coming from London or further by rail. Birdwatching is one draw and it is in contrast with interest in birds a century back. Clifford Musgrave writes: 'An extraordinary aspect of Brighton life in Edwardian days was the activities of the bird-catchers. A number of families specialised in this traffic. Every morning in the season some twenty or thirty men went out from Brighton on to the Downs, where they set nets to catch birds of all kinds. Larks and wheatears were sold as delicacies to the big hotels. Singing birds were kept alive and sold in cages' (19). Today visitors from Brighton to the Downs are delighted by birdsong seen though as part of the uncapturable beauty of the hills above.

Exiting the ticket barrier at Brighton Station turn left then left again past the cycle storage and taxi rank onto Stroudley Road.

Descend the stairs and cross New England Street into Ann Street down to London Road. Cross into Oxford Street continuing across Ditchling Road into The Level heading diagonally left at the public toilets to the corner of the park. Cross Union Road and go straight ahead along Lewes Road past St Martin's Church. Cross the road and enter the Cemetery just before The Gladstone Pub. On Sundays the cemetery opens later at 11am. Continue towards Woodvale Crematorium following the road left up to Bear Road. Cross the road and turn right to walk up beside the City Cemetery walls. When you reach the top of Bear Road take the farm track to the left parallel to Warren Road which continues above Brighton Racecourse. After this becomes a cycle track, keep right at the junction and continue north of Woodingdean.

Cross Falmer Road with care into Drove Avenue to walk across the South Downs. At the junction after the telecommunications mast on Newmarket Hill keep right after which you enter the ancient Jugg's Road (track). After a short distance SDW joins this track from the left and you leave Jugg's Road to head right along SDW. Enjoy views to the left of Lewes, Mount Caburn and the Radio Station above Glynde. SDW twists and turns heading upward to reveal a splendid view to the left of Seven Sisters and Seaford Head on the coastal horizon with Newhaven and Peacehaven radio mast to your right. SDW heads right then left onto a cemented track heading towards the striking Newhaven Energy Recovery Facility.

Continue straight on SDW leaving the concrete road. Turn left off SDW down to Rodmell village where you can spend time at The Abergavenny Arms before continuing to catch the hourly train from Southease back to Brighton. A horseshoe detour is recommended from the pub to St Peter's Church and the Monk's House associated with the modernist author Virginia Wolff and the artistic and literary Bloomsbury Group. In 1941 Virginia (59) drowned herself in the adjacent River Ouse. You return to Piddinghoe Road taking the permissive footpath just before the main road which runs parallel to it to Southease and joins SDW. Bear left in the village, taking a detour right to Southease Church with its round stone tower, rejoining SDW to follow the road across the Ouse to Southease railway station.

8.3 mile/13.3 km

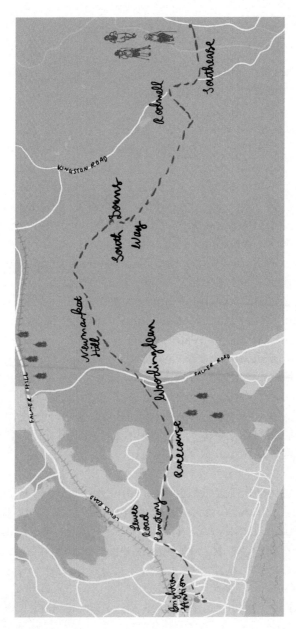

Southease

Rodmell

KINGSTON ROAD

South Downs Way

Newmarket Hill

Woodingdean

FALMER ROAD

FALMER HILL

Racecourse

LEWES ROAD

Lewes Road

Bevendean

Brighton Station

22   Ovingdean

9 mile circular walk via Brighton Racecourse to Ovingdean returning via the Undercliff Walk

The character of Ovingdean village survived the eastward expansion of Brighton from the 1920s. By contrast Whitehawk's smallholdings and allotments gave way to a new estate built in the wake of slum clearances in Brighton to rehouse thousands of people. Ovingdean expanded modestly. Though absorbed into the administrative borough of Brighton in 1928, it remains insulated from Whitehawk and the city west of it by a swathe of green. This includes the cemeteries, racecourse and golf course making the village an attractive destination for a walk from Brighton & Hove with stunning coastal views. St Wulfran's Church in Ovingdean is mentioned in the Domesday Book (1086). A Victorian restoration involved famous villager, stained glass designer Charles Eamer Kempe (1837-1907) who decorated the chancel panelling, provided seven windows and designed the rood screen carved in Oberammergau. Kempe is buried in St Wulfran's Churchyard as is electrical engineer Magnus Volk (1851-1937) who designed and built the Volk's electric railway running from Brighton Pier to the Marina.

Exiting the ticket barrier at Brighton Station turn left then left again past the cycle storage past the taxi rank onto Stroudley Road. Descend the stairs to the right of the roundabout and cross Fleet Street into Fenchurch Walk and then New England Street into Ann Street. The walk passes right of St Bartholomew's Church down to London Road. Cross into Oxford Street continuing past the Bat & Ball pub across

Ditchling Road into The Level heading diagonally left at the public toilets to the north-east corner of the park. Cross Union Road and proceed straight ahead along Gladstone Terrace and Lewes Road past St Martin's Church with its military associations. Cross Lewes Road before the Gyratory to enter Lewes Road Cemetery just before The Gladstone Pub. On Sundays and Bank Holidays the cemetery opens later at 11am. Continue up past the Coroner's Court to Woodvale Crematorium where there are public toilets. The stained glass windows in the North Chapel are worth a detour. Follow the way left up to Bear Road noting the statue of the life-sized circus pony in mourning on top of John Ginnett's tomb (1892).

At Bear Road turn right continuing up along the pavement to cross the access road to Downs Crematorium and top of Tenantry Down Road into the footpath. This path crosses the access road to the car park continuing parallel to Bear Road past seats from which you can enjoy coastal views of the city. Head for the gate to the left of the bus stop sign visible at the top of the hill. With care cross Wilson Avenue and continue in the same direction to the left of the bus stop through a gate, across the grassed race course and then through another gate. Turn left and follow the public bridleway parallel to the race course. Cross the main road with care continuing along the bridleway enjoying scenic views of the coast. At the footpath junction head left across the race course into the car park.

Turn right and head into the signed path alongside the 'Gallup' where the racecourse descends from the hill. The walk descends on a rough path to the left of the golf course with Roedean School and St Dunstans Blind Veteran Centre on the horizon to the 12th century Church St Wulfran in Ovingdean. Take a short detour to view the Church before continuing along Greenways past St Dunstan's into the underpass, down the steps and right to Ovingdean cafe and the public toilets. Continue along the Undercliff Walk to Brighton Marina enjoying bracing sea winds and waves. The route continues at the end of the Under Cliff Walk straight ahead up the slope under the road and down to the right of Black Rock electric rail terminal. Continue along Madeira Drive and past the pier along King's Road then down the slope continuing along the Esplanade. Turn right after the toilets into the underpass which emerges at the bottom of West Street. Walk up to the Clock Tower and up Queen's Road to Brighton railway station.

9.1 mile/14.6 km

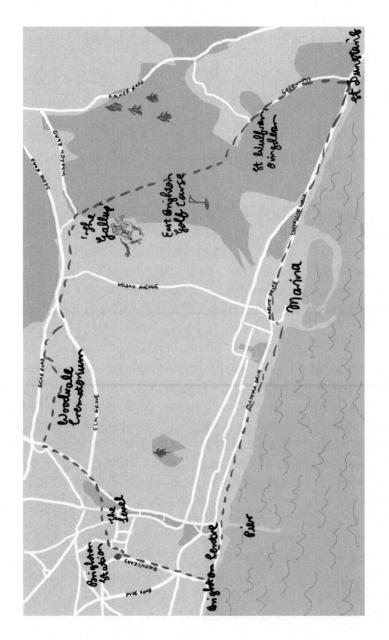

FALMER ROAD

GREENWAYS

St Dunstan's

St Wulfran's Ovingdean

East Brighton Golf Course

DROVE ROAD

WARREN ROAD

'the gallops'

UNDERCLIFF WALK

Marina

WILSON AVENUE

MARINE DRIVE

Woodvale Crematorium

BEAR ROAD

ELM GROVE

MADEIRA DRIVE

the Level

Pier

Brighton Station

Brighton Centre

QUEEN'S ROAD

DYKE ROAD

23   Chattri Memorial

11 mile circular walk via Preston Park to Chattri Memorial returning via Hollingbury Camp

During World War One (1914-1918), Clifford Musgrave writes, 'the Royal Pavilion housed wounded soldiers of many different castes and religions, who lived amicably together with the aid of nine separate kitchens, duplicate water taps in every ward, and multilingual notices. More than one account has survived of Indian soldiers being brought in unconscious, waking up amid the fantastic oriental decorations of the ceiling in the Music Room or Banqueting Room, and imagining they had died and were waking in Paradise. In this way the Royal Pavilion achieved a romantic fulfilment beyond the wildest imaginings of its original creators. There was also a less poetical side to this episode. A high wooden fence had been built around the Pavilion grounds to ensure privacy, and it was considered "worth a penny to take a ride on the trams along the Steine to get a glimpse of the Indians in the grounds"... the Chattri, a small domed monument on the Downs near Patcham is dedicated to the memory of the Indians who died at the Pavilion, and built on the sight of the burning *ghat* where there bodies were cremated. Pilgrims continue to be made to this day and commemorative services held there by visiting Indians' (20).

Exiting the ticket barrier at Brighton Station turn left then left again past the cycle storage and taxi rank onto Stroudley Road. Continue past the steps to enter Brighton Greenway on the old railway track. Descend to New England Road, turn left under the bridge and left down Argyle Road continuing to its junction with Preston Road. Turn left continuing under the viaduct and walk across the pedestrian crossings into Preston Park. Join the path to the right of the Rose Garden. Continue straight ahead keeping to the right of the Play Park. After the Clock Tower head half right towards the car park and enter the path between the hedges leading to Preston Park Gate.

Continue in the same direction walking across Preston Drove on the zebra crossing onto Surrenden Road. After Harrington Road cross to join the path on the wooded island in the centre of the dual carriageway. Continue right along this island at the junction with Surrenden Crescent. You keep Varndean College fields on your right. After the second junction with Surrenden Crescent the island disappears. Take the left hand pavement as the long gentle incline continues. The road merges with Braybon Avenue at the top where you can enjoy scenic views of the Downs ahead. Continue along and then down Braybon Avenue. After St Thomas More Church turn left along Carden Avenue. Turn right at the shops proceeding along Patchdean to the Clock Tower where the walk proceeds half left up Vale Avenue. Cross Vale Road opposite Patcham Court Farmhouse and continue on the footpath to just beyond the traffic island. Cross and head in the same direction across the road bridge. Continue across the A27 slip road, turn left and walk to the right up the road then left onto the Sussex Border Path (SBP) heading up onto the South Downs.

Take a right detour to visit the Chattri. After returning to SBP continue north passing a copse on your left and walk down through a large gate. Take a right turn leaving SBP and continue on the path beside the wire fence. Turn right at the gate and head past the brick barn. The farm track veers left, passing a larger barn and footpath junction. Continue in the same direction down through Lower Standean farm past the cow shed, farm cottages and another cow shed up the slope to Wonderhill Plantation where the walk heads left up to the scenic New Barn. 1,500 acre Standean farm, mixing arable, beef cattle, pigs and sheep, has been farmed by the Carnaghan family for almost a century. At New Barn head right through the gate continuing up along the track. The Chattri memorial is visible to your right. After the left bend continue under electric cables to Ditchling Road. Cross through the gate to the right of the old dew pond, where there is a bus stop, into Piddingworth Plantation, Stanmer Park. Go through the gate immediately to your right heading left along the main footpath which curves right continuing alongside a row of hedges with Ditching Road to the right. Falmer Stadium appears in the far distance on your left. The path reaches a concreted section then passes through a gate into the wood. Continue, crossing the metalled road to Stanmer Village, and then take the right fork. Continue through the wood taking a right turn at the end to pass through the gap in the wall down to Coldean Lane. Cross with care via the traffic island and continue across the A27 beside Ditchling Road. Cross onto the joint pedestrian/cycleway heading toward Brighton. Approaching Hollingbury cross Ditchling Road into the second car park entrance and turn right along the footpath nearest the hedge heading to Hollingbury Golf Course and then left of that into the wood. Turn right at the first junction and walk around the golf tee then right continuing straight ahead to the Iron Age hill fort (450BC or so) known as Hollingbury Camp (or Castle).

Walk around the shallow walls of the tumulus with its trig point enjoying views of Brighton & Hove and the South Downs.

Head back to the wood via the golf tee. At the path crossing with the display board turn right and continue as the path bends to and fro before reaching the T at the break in the hedge. Take a detour left to view the Dewpond then head back to follow the path with a sea view along the hedge to the right of the large field. Proceed through the car park and then to the left of the football pitch and playground of Hollingdean Park. At Lynchet Close turn right and at the Community Centre take a left turn onto Brentswood Road. Turn right at the junction descending Stephens Road to The Crossway. Turn left then right down Horton Road enjoying the sea view ahead. At the T junction turn right onto Davey Drive then left on reaching Upper Hollingdean Road. Take the first right cutting onto Hollingdean Lane. Turn right to walk beside Hollingdean's Material Recovery Facility and Waste Transfer Station with its signal dragonflies bearing left back up onto Ditchling Road. Take a left turn and continue down to The Level with St Peter's Church on the horizon. Turn right at the Bat & Ball pub to walk along Oxford Street to London Road. Cross and enter Ann Street. Continue past St Bartholomew's Church and School up the stairs back to Brighton Station.

10.7 mile/17.2 km

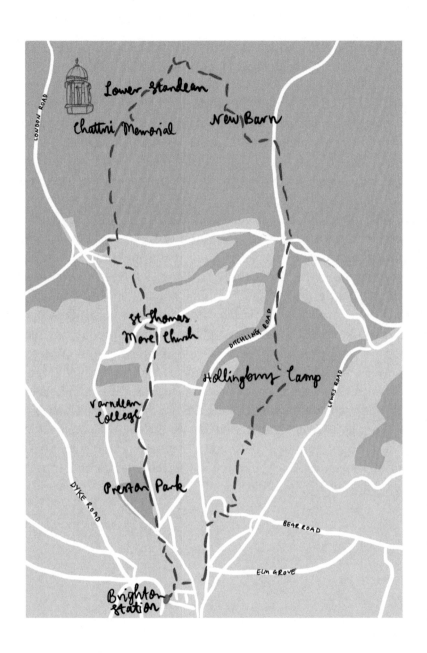

Lower Standean

Chattri Memorial

New Barn

St Thomas More Church

Ditchling Road

Hollingbury Camp

Lewes Road

Varndean College

London Road

Dyke Road

Preston Park

Bear Road

Elm Grove

Brighton Station

125

24   Newhaven

*11 mile seaside and cliff walk via Peacehaven Meridian
Monument to Newhaven returning via bus or train*

The River Ouse causes a gap in the South Downs east of
Brighton & Hove and Newhaven, now the natural eastern
perimeter of the city, lies at its mouth. It is called 'new' haven
because it replaced Seaford, main outlet and former 'Cinque
Port' of the Ouse in the Middle Ages, due to the shifting of sand
banks over the centuries. 'Newhaven-Dieppe is the oldest of the
cross-channel routes. William the Conqueror is said to have set
off from Dieppe on his second trip to England, conquered the
year before in 1066. At the start of the 19th century, boats from
Dieppe anchored off Brighton, with passengers landed by small
boats. A pier to make disembarkation easier didn't appear until
1823... In 1824 the General Steam Navigation Company linked
England to Dieppe using paddle steamers with a length of 25
metres... taking nine hours twice a week' (21). Brighton gave
way to Newhaven as a ferry terminus better equipped for such
large boats once its sheltered harbour came into use coincident
with the railway's arrival in 1847. The low-water port at
Newhaven is the only such port between Dover and Portsmouth
open to shipping at all times. This walk from Brighton to
Newhaven keeps to promenades, cliff tops or under cliff paths
and passes the Meridian monument at Peacehaven.

From the forecourt of Brighton Station walk down Queen's
Road to the Clock Tower. Cross North Street and continue
down West Street on the right hand pavement. At King's Road
you follow the invitation 'Descend subway to beach'. After the

toilets turn left to proceed along the Esplanade and eventually up the slope onto Kings Road heading past the pier. Continue to the right of the Aquarium onto Madeira Drive and walk along the promenade. After the Black Rock miniature railway terminal continue straight ahead up the slope keeping to the right beside the cycle track on the pavement by the fence. Descend the slope which joins the Undercliff Walk and pass through the metal gates. Walk to the left of the supermarket passing the Marina yacht basin and housing, boatyard and promenade entrance. At Ovingdean beach there are toilets and a cafe. At Rottingdean beach you pass under the Quarterdeck Promontory to another cafe with toilets and the hard path continues to Saltdean. After passing White Cliffs Cafe, turn left up the slope following the signed England Coast Path (ECP) up to the bus stop which is diagonally across from Saltdean Lido.

Turn right walking past the seats and continue along the cliff top. Head up alongside the wire fence passing the ECP path sign and the weather vane erected 1995 to mark 50 years from the end of the Second World War. Head through the gate signed ECP diagonally left across the field and then across the tarmac road up to the left of the Water Works gates. The path continues towards Smugglers Rest pub. Go through the gate and turn right heading down to the cliff top enjoying the view and the rabbits. Continue beside the fence passing in front of housing on The Esplanade, Telscombe after which house addresses are on The Promenade, Peacehaven. Follow ECP across Howard Park where there is an option on the right to follow the Under Cliff pathway. Walk along The Promenade and across The Dell, well used for community events, to the King George V memorial erected 1936 marking Peacehaven's position on the Greenwich

Meridian. King George and Queen Mary were regular visitors to the south coast.

At Bastion Steps from the Under Cliff path continue on ECP along The Promenade. At the end of the houses Newhaven Harbour and Seaford Head come into view as the path heads left past steps down to another Under Cliff path, an alternative route for walking into Newhaven. Continue carefully on the cliff top along ECP, initially alongside the wire fence and then choosing paths close to the cliff top and down across the wooden bridge. ECP continues up Castle Hill to a military bunker and Newhaven lookout (2004) 175 ft (53 m) above sea level beside the radio mast which has exclusive use of VHF Channel 65 used by seafarers. There was a fort on Castle Hill in the Bronze Age. Continue to the right of the lookout past another bunker then left on ECP as signed then right onto a metalled road which continues down through the car park to the drawbridge of Newhaven Fort. Constructed with concrete in the 19th century at a time of tension in Anglo-French relations it was built into the contours of the land rather above ground like a traditional fort or castle. The Fort is open seasonally. Enjoy the panoramic view of Newhaven Harbour and Seaford Bay from its entrance. Descend from there down Fort Rise through Castle Hill Nature Reserve and at the bottom continue left between recreation ground and Marina then heading right as signed on ESP. The Marina jetty on the right has memorials for the centenary of the UK arrival of famous Vietnamese Ho Chi Minh (1913) and tragic drowning of two fishermen in 2020. Continue left on ESP past Lifeboat and Market buildings and Ark pub. At the junction with the main road turn left to catch a

12 bus or right across the swing bridge to catch a train from Newhaven Town station back to Brighton Station.

11.1 mile/17.8 km

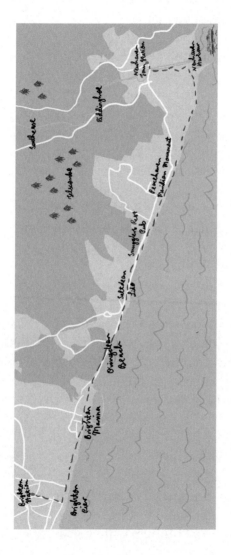

25   Bramber Castle

11 mile walk via Portslade and Monarch's Way to Bramber Castle returning by bus

Main access to Brighton & Hove from the north is by road or rail exploiting the lowering of the South Downs at Pyecombe. Further west there is an actual gap in the hills serving the River Adur's access to the sea which makes a natural boundary to the city. Steyning town, former port, with the villages of Bramber and Upper Beeding sit at the crossing-point of the river now exploited by the South Downs Way. Bramber Castle, seat of the de Braose family, was built at the Norman Conquest to defend this crossing. The one surviving wall of the tower, standing 46 foot (14 metres) high, indicates how imposing it once was before subsidence led to its ruin in the 16th century. Two centuries before Steyning had declined as the Adur began to silt up causing the town to lose trade and population. Shoreham-by-Sea, 4 miles (6.4 km) down river, succeeded it as port. One Brighton link is the colourful Anglo Saxon hermit St Cuthman of Steyning, also patron of Whitehawk Church. 'Historical facts about St Cuthman are few. The Saxon port at Steyning was called Cuthman's Port... The legend... that Chanctonbury Ring was created by the Devil who had decided one night to excavate a channel from the sea to drown the Christians of Sussex. Cuthman foiled the plan by holding a candle under a colander and knocking a cock off its perch. When the Devil saw the light and heard the cock crow he fled, leaving his plan unfinished except for the creation of the South Downs from Chanctonbury Ring to 'Devil's Dyke.' We cannot be sure exactly where Cuthman's life began except that the story, handed down over generations, says he walked from West to East Sussex with his mother in a wheeled bed like a wheelbarrow' (22). This walk from Brighton Station could be shortened to 5 mile/8 km by starting from Fishersgate Station.

Exiting the ticket barrier at Brighton Station turn left then left again past the cycle storage and taxi rank onto Stroudley Road. Continue past the steps to enter Brighton Greenway which follows an old railway track. Descend to New England Road, turn left under the bridge and left down Argyle Street continuing to its junction with Preston Road. Turn left continuing under the viaduct and walk across the pedestrian crossings into Preston Park. Head half right through the Rose Garden to Rotunda Cafe and toilets then left to walk between the tennis courts. Head right then left towards Chalet Cafe and then veer left following the path with St Peter's Church, Preston Manor and Garden to the right. Re-entering the pavement of Preston Road turn right then left across the pedestrian crossing by the Petrol Station and walk up South Road. Passing under the railway bridge with the PDSA Pets Hospital to your right, continue straight ahead up the steep incline of The Drove to cross Dyke Road.

Keep straight ahead along The Droveway. After crossing Shirley Drive continue along the wooded pavement. At the junction with Goldstone Crescent go straight into Hove Park and turn left along the pedestrian way walking parallel to the Crescent. The walk continues past the playground and tennis courts to the Park entrance on Old Shoreham Road. Turn right onto the pavement. Cross Nevill Road via the pedestrian crossing and continue in the same direction passing the sign pointing left to

Aldrington Station. Cross Old Shoreham Road at the pedestrian crossing before Holmes Avenue. Continue walking and turn left into the southern section of Hove Cemetery, immediately right, past the public toilet, proceeding along the road between the graves. Turn right at the junction returning to Old Shoreham Road. Head left then left down Olive Road over the railway bridge and down to the junction with Portland Road. Turn right and walk past Portslade Station after which there are public toilets before the level crossing. Cross the railway and turn left at The Victoria Pub along Victoria Road. After Portslade Town Hall take the signed left turn opposite the recreation ground into Portslade Cemetery. Turn right at the road junction and continue past the Cemetery Chapel to the exit.

Cross the road and descend Shelldale Road to the West Sussex sign by the left turn to Fishersgate station. Take a right turn into the footpath opposite and continue past the allotments and Fishersgate electric substation to Old Shoreham Road. Cross with the Southwick sign to the left into the continuation of the tarmac footpath walking beside the pylons along the boundary between East and West Sussex. Continue across Mile Oak Road up into the third section of footpath and then across Mile Oak Gardens by the green triangle into another section which enters a bridleway beside a recreation ground. Continue on the path between the trees heading right at the end of the recreation ground where, looking back, views open up of Shoreham Power station and the turbines out to sea. At the fence go through the gate heading half left walking just to the left of the left hand pylon to the footpath sign. Continue in the direction signed with Mile Oak down to the right. The route continues straight as signed at the footpath junction sign, heading up the public bridleway with the pylons now below and well to the right. The hum of A27 traffic exiting Southwick tunnel below is evident. Continue straight up on the grass over the chalk track heading left to right across your route. There is a seat above the tunnel before the path heads slightly left. Look back from there to the left at Foredown Tower, converted Edwardian water tower housing a camera obscura, perched on the opposite ridge. Continue on the broad path through the gorse bushes keeping to the left. When the path flattens head left through one of the gates onto a well defined track beside a wire fence. Worthing with its Bayside tower block is down to the left. On the right the pylon line is seen to cross the Downs at Fulking escarpment.

At the gate turn left as signed continuing on Monarch's Way passing an extensive hard standing. Charles Stuart was chased along this path in 1651 having encountered Puritan soldiers at Bramber on his way to catch a boat to France from Shoreham and escape the country after his father's execution. Continue on the path enjoying the view across the Adur to Lancing College Chapel (1868) built in striking gothic revival style. The more prosaic chimney of the redundant Beeding Cement Works lies below on the near side of the River Adur. At Beeding Hill car park cross SDW descending Monarch's Way as signed. The last section of the path merges with The Bostal. At the bottom turn left along the pavement of Henfield Road passing Steyning Grammar School along A2037. Turn right at the roundabout bearing left after the petrol station passing the King's Head pub (1788) to walk across the River Adur bridge into Bramber. Walk on past St Mary's House (1470) associated with Knights Templar. At the Old Tollgate Hotel cross and walk up the steps past St Nicholas's Church to Bramber Castle (1073). After visiting the stone and mound the walk can be extended along the road to Steyning. Head back into Bramber to catch a 2 bus back to Churchill Square from where you walk past the Clock Tower up Queen's Road to Brighton Station.

11.2 mile/18.0 km

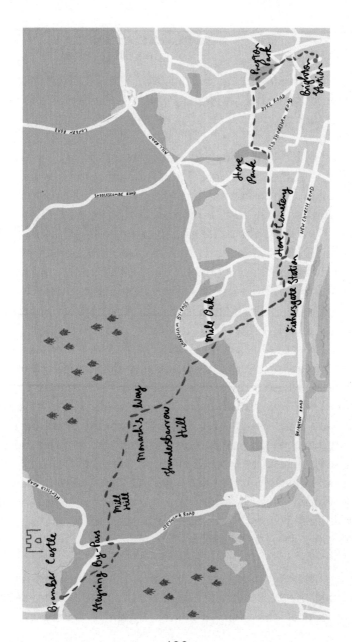

Bramber Castle

Steyning By-Pass

Mill Hill

Monarch's Way

Thundersbarrow Hill

Mile Oak

Hove Park

Preston Park

Brighton Station

Hove Cemetery

Fishersgate Station

HENFIELD ROAD

STEYNING ROAD

SHOREHAM BYPASS

BRIGHTON ROAD

NEW CHURCH ROAD

OLD SHOREHAM ROAD

DYKE ROAD

SADDLESCOMBE ROAD

MILL ROAD

LONDON ROAD

26   Shoreham Port

11.5 mile circular walk via Preston Park, Hove Park and Southwick Park to Shoreham Port returning via the seaside road, Hove Lagoon and Brighton Promenade.

The Monarch's Way runs 625 miles (1005 km) in repeated zig zags from Worcester to Shoreham. It commemorates the escape by boat from Shoreham to France of the Prince of Wales, later King Charles II in 1651 after the Battle of Worcester in the English Civil War. The route established 1994 by Trevor Antill is maintained by Monarch's Way Association in partnership with local authorities. 'Passing to the south of Steyning it crosses the River Adur at Bramber to Upper Beeding. After crossing Beeding Hill and Thundersbarrow Hill the path approaches the northern edge of the built-up area near Mile Oak, before doubling sharply back to the north of the A27 to continue east across the downs, before heading south down the former route of the Devil's Dyke railway towards West Blatchington. Crossing the built-up area south-eastwards towards Hove, it crosses Hove Park near Brighton & Hove Greyhound Stadium, before zig-zagging through the streets of Brighton to Brighton Pier. From here it runs westwards along the sea-front through Hove and Portslade, to Shoreham-by-Sea' (23). The Southwick Ship Canal visited on this walk runs parallel with the shoreline alongside Shoreham Power Station hosting ships that approach Shoreham Port past the harbour.

Exiting the ticket barrier at Brighton Station turn left then left again past the cycle storage and taxi rank onto Stroudley Road. Continue past the steps to enter Brighton Greenway which follows an old railway track. Descend to New England Road, turn left under the bridge and left down Argyle Street continuing to its junction with Preston Road. Turn left continuing under the viaduct and walk across the pedestrian crossings into Preston Park. Head half right through the Rose Garden to Rotunda Cafe and toilets then left to walk between the tennis courts. Head right then left towards Chalet Cafe and then veer left following the path to re-enter the pavement of Preston Road. Turn right then left across the pedestrian crossing by the Petrol Station and walk up South Road. Passing under the railway bridge continue straight ahead up the steep incline of The Drove to cross Dyke Road. Keep straight ahead along The Droveway where on the left pavement you pass The Bishop's House used by Bishops of Chichester during the Second World War. Cross Shirley Drive and continue along the wooded pavement.

At the junction with Goldstone Crescent go straight into Hove Park and turn left along the pedestrian way walking parallel to the Crescent. The walk crosses here a section of Monarch's Way then continues past the playground and tennis courts to the Park entrance on Old Shoreham Road. Turn right onto the pavement. Cross Nevill Road via the pedestrian crossing and continue in the same direction passing the sign pointing left to Aldrington Station. Cross Old Shoreham Road at the pedestrian crossing before Holmes Avenue. Continue walking and turn left into the southern section of Hove Cemetery, immediately right, past the public toilet, proceeding along the road between the graves. Turn right at the junction returning to the main road opposite the entrance to the northern section of Hove Cemetery which may merit a detour. Turn left along Old Shoreham Road then left down Olive Road over the railway bridge and down to the junction with Portland Road. Turn right and walk past Portslade Station after which there are public toilets before the level crossing.

Cross the railway and turn left at The Victoria Pub along Victoria Road. After Portslade Town Hall take the signed left turn opposite the recreation ground into Portslade Cemetery. Turn right at the road junction and continue past the Cemetery Chapel to the exit. Cross the road and descend Shelldale Road which becomes Manor Hall Road. After the Steyning bus stop and seat turn left into Old Barn Way signed for the Leisure Centre. Turn right before Southwick Football Club into the path to Southwick Leisure Centre and head to the left of the building into Southwick Park. Cross diagonally to the park exit into Croft Avenue. At the junction with Southwick Street turn left and continue past Southwick Station under the railway bridge past the roundabout to Albion Street. Turn right then cross the pedestrian crossing, which has an adjacent footpath sign, into the access road to Shoreham Port.

Continue across the lock gates enjoying views of the ship canal under the towering edifice of Shoreham Power Station. Continue along Basin Road South and head across the zebra crossing onto the promenade which is the last section of Monarch's Way. The walk can detour here to Shoreham Harbour near the place Charles Stuart boarded the 'Surprise' at 2 am on 15 October 1651 sailing on the high tide five hours later. Two hours after he sailed soldiers arrived belatedly in Shoreham to arrest him. Continue left along the promenade past Carat's Cafe and public toilets enjoying the sea view. The walk returns to Basin Road South for a stretch where you capture the commercial importance of the Port.

There are opportunities to go back onto the sea walls and banks before the road bends left at the car park and right to Hove Lagoon. At the left turn head right off Basin Road South then onto the Promenade walking above the Lagoon past the beach huts. Enjoy the sea view continuing past public toilets to King Alfred Leisure Centre onto King's Esplanade knowing Charles Stuart once fled in the opposite direction along this seafront, now labelled Monarch's Way, to Shoreham. There are public toilets off Hove Lawns as you continue to the Peace Statue. Continue past Brighton Beach Bandstand and the i360 viewing tower. The walk ascends up West Street to the Clock Tower and continues up Queen's Road back to Brighton Station forecourt.

11.5 mile/18.6 km

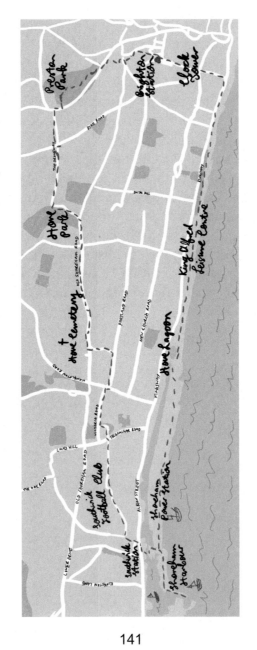

27 Rottingdean

12 mile circular walk via Brighton Racecourse to Rottingdean returning via Undercliff Walk

'In the High and Far off Times, the Elephant ... had no trunk,' wrote Rottingdean resident Rudyard Kipling. 'He had just a blackish, bulgy nose, as big as a boot, that he could wriggle about from side to side'. But there was one elephant's child who was more curious than the rest. He wanted to know what the crocodile had for dinner. Since no one would tell him, he went down to the banks of the Limpopo to find out for himself. When he bent down to see, the crocodile bit his nose – and pulled until it was 'nearly five feet long'. That, Kipling smiled, was how the elephant got its trunk' (24). This 'Just So' story was written during Kipling's time at The Elms (1897-1902) living adjacent to his father-in-law Pre-Raphaelite painter Edward Burne-Jones (1833-1898) at Prospect House, Rottingdean. This picturesque village has drawn and inspired writers and painters over centuries benefiting from the proximity of Brighton as a creative hub alongside the intimacy of village life. At its restoration St Margaret's Church received windows built by William Morris to the designs of Edward Burne-Jones. The beauty of Rottingdean Church so impacted some American visitors that a replica of it was constructed 1941 at the Forest Lawn Memorial Park, Glendale, California.

Exiting the ticket barrier at Brighton Station turn left then left again past the cycle storage and taxi rank onto Stroudley Road. Descend the stairs and cross New England Street into Ann Street down to London Road. Cross into Oxford Street continuing across Ditchling Road into The Level heading diagonally left at the public toilets to the corner of the park. Cross Union Road and go straight ahead along Lewes Road past St Martin's Church. Cross the road and enter the Cemetery just before The Gladstone Pub. On Sundays and Bank Holidays the cemetery opens later at 11am. Continue towards Woodvale Crematorium following the road left up to Bear Road. Cross the road and turn right walking up on the pavement beside the City Cemetery walls. At the top of Bear Road continue opposite the Racecourse along Warren Road. After the traffic lights head left down steps then right along the farm track which joins a bridleway.

Continue in the same direction keeping right at the junction walking to the left of the bungalows passing Drove Road Stud on your left. Cross Falmer Road with care and continue straight ahead on the signed bridleway passing to the right of the two metal gates and following the path as it curves right. At the junction before the transmitter keep right and continue past the reservoir. At the path junction take the right fork continuing alongside the fence. As the walk descends, enjoy the sea view. Peacehaven, Newhaven, Seaford Head and Seven Sisters appear to the left on the horizon and St Dunstan's Blind Veteran Centre, Ovingdean to the right. Before Balsdean Reservoir head left, cross the road and continue on the bridleway. After the gate continue straight ahead beside the hedge past Balsdean Cottages. Continue, veering left after the gate, viewing Rottingdean windmill on the cliff to your right and the colony of contemporary windmills at sea to the left on the horizon. On arrival at Bishopstone Drive turn right, continue on the byway and head downhill to the right ignoring the right hand turn.

After passing the top of Chailey Avenue continue down Whiteway Lane past the school, Our Lady of Lourdes Roman Catholic Church and Library to Vicarage Lane. Turn right walking past The Plough pub and village pond to the full sized Lych Gate inviting a detour to view St Margaret of Antioch Church tracing back to Saxon times. Cross the village green past the war memorial to view The Elms, home to Rudyard Kipling and Prospect House home to Edward Burne-Jones. Turn left along the High Street, cross A259 and continue past White Horse pub and Quarterdeck Promontory onto the Undercliff Walk. Enjoy bracing sea winds and waves as you return to Brighton via the Marina, Madeira Drive and the Esplanade. Cross at the pedestrian crossing to head up West Street then past the Clock Tower up Queen's Road to Brighton railway station.

11.9 mile/19.2 km

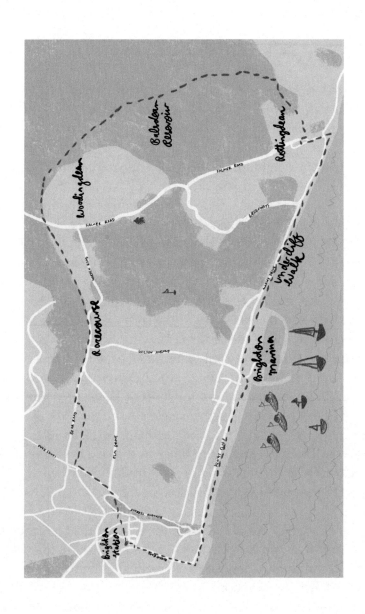

Balsdean Reservoir

Rottingdean

FALMER ROAD

GREENWAYS

FALMER ROAD

Undercliff Walk

MARINE DRIVE

Racecourse

WILSON AVENUE

Brighton Marina

BEAR ROAD

ELM GROVE

KING'S CLIFF

LONG'S ROAD

RICHMOND TERRACE

Brighton Station

QUEEN'S ROAD

146

28   Ditchling Beacon

13.5 mile circular walk via Hollingbury Camp to Ditchling Beacon returning via Sussex Border Path, Patcham and Withdean Park

In June 1514 Brighton was virtually burned to the ground by French raiders eventually repelled by archers from across Sussex who sped to the scene alerted by fires lit on the Downs. Ditchling Beacon is associated with this event and was part of a chain of beacons warning in 1587 of the approach of the Spanish Armada. In recent years fires have been kindled to celebrate events such as the Queen's Jubilee. Ditchling Beacon is the highest point in East Sussex with an elevation of 814 foot (248 meter) with spectacular views of the coast, across Sussex Weald and east-west along the Downs. The site was an Iron Age hill fort and its ramparts are still detectable, especially those facing north. The fort would dominate adjoining parts of the ridge and the much lower ground to the north. It was a large camp enclosing 13.6 acres (5.5 hectares). In the Middle Ages swineherds from Brighton and Patcham, preferring the drier route over Ditchling Beacon to those west along the Adur or east along the Ouse, hollowed out paths driving their pigs over the Downs to pasture at Wivelsfield and beyond.

Exiting the ticket barrier at Brighton Station turn left then left again past the cycle storage and taxi rank onto Stroudley Road. Descend the stairs and cross New England Street into Ann Street down to London Road. Cross into Oxford Street continuing from the Bat & Ball pub across Ditchling Road and walk left along the pavement beside The Level. Cross Union

Road at the pedestrian crossing and continue up Ditchling Road. Turn right after the petrol station along Hollingdean Lane walking past the Material Recovery Facility and Waste Transfer Station with its decorative dragonflies on the right by the mini roundabout. Head left at this roundabout and left along Upper Hollingdean Road, first right along Davey Drive then first left up Horton Road. At The Crossway turn left then first right up Stephens Road. Take a left turn up Brentwood Road then right along Lynchet Close past Hollingdean Children's Centre and the sign for Hollingdean Park.

Turn left along the signed public footpath and follow the semi metalled track past the skate park and football ground through the car park onto the signed gravelled path. As you walk up the edge of the field the houses of Moulsecoomb and Falmer Stadium appear on the right. Look back across the city taking in the sea view. Hollingbury Golf Course appears on the left through the bushes. University buildings appear in the valley to the right. When the path bends left, continue straight ahead to view the Dewpond. Return to the path you were on and, turning left on it, head between the bushes onto the track. Hollingbury Camp is visible as this track bears right. Divert on the bend through the gate and permissive footpath to view the square sided fort (450-250 BC) used as a beacon from the middle ages onwards. Return to the track which continues along the wire fence around the golf course. Continue straight at the footpath junction sign below Hole 12.

The path emerges from the wood giving a choice of paths over the field to the right of the golf course. Continue parallel to the hedge. At the car park turn left down the short access road and cross Ditchling Road onto the footpath shared with cyclists. Turn right and head along beside the road. Just before the bridge over the A27 cross to the pavement on the other side of Ditchling Road. Continue over the bridge, cross the slip road via the traffic island and head up into the wood past the railing and footpath sign and through the gap in the wall. Walk to the adjacent footpath junction and turn left to follow the well defined track through the wood. Go straight, as signed to South Downs Way (SDW), across the access road into Stanmer and follow immediately the left fork onto the main track through the wood.

On exiting the wood continue along the concrete standing and head in the same direction beside the bushes. The path bears left toward gates. Go through the gate giving access to the path running immediately right of Ditchling Road. The dome of the Chattri memorial is visible to the right in the far distance. After the old dew pond head through the left hand gate into the wood continuing parallel to the road. Take the left fork to the road when signed at High Park Corner. Cross the road at the bus stop. The 79 bus to Brighton & Hove operates at weekends and on bank holidays.

Continue on the bridleway beside the fence. Go through a gate and continue right along the fence which runs initially parallel to the road as it skirts the valley to the left. After being joined from the left by the pathway up the valley the path continues up a stony track between wire fences. Towards the brow of the hill turn right through the metal gate and follow the track which crosses a large field. Turn left at the footpath sign and continue beside the low embankment which runs parallel to Ditchling

Road. SDW from Lewes appears above to the right and Mid Sussex beyond the Downs ridge the way sits on. Go through the gate at the top of the field and continue straight ahead beside the fence. Turn left to follow the fence to the trig point at Ditchling Beacon. Trig points or triangulation stations are concrete pillars used in surveying land placed at highest points on hills and mountains.

Follow the fence to the right of the trig point down to SDW. A diversion right to the car park beyond the gate is a possibility where an ice cream van is regular visitor in summer. Head left along SDW enjoying views across Sussex and the sea. The Sussex Border Path (SBP) joins the path from the right before a gate. After the gate note the 'Keymer Post' indicating the intersection of Winchester-Eastbourne and Keymer-Brighton routes. The former towns start and finish the 100 mile (161 km) SDW. Turn left off SDW continuing as signed on SBP to Brighton down alongside the wire fence. The path is also signed to Chattri Memorial. Enjoy views to the right of Devil's Dyke's masts with Pyecombe and its golf course in the foreground and, to the left, Ditchling Road and the houses of Brighton & Hove overlooked by the i360 tower. At the footpath crossing by the metal gates continue straight ahead. Shortly after the copse the Chattri appears to the left of your descent. This is a memorial to Hindu and Sikh Indian soldiers, previously hospitalised in Brighton's Dome, who died and were cremated here on the Downs.

Continuing down from the Chattri, keep straight heading for i360 on the horizon. Pass through the gate under the electric wires as the hum of traffic ascends from the A27. At the car park turn right along the road and follow the pavement round. Cross the A27 slip road to the left of the grassed roundabout heading for the Lewes sign. Continue on the pavement across the A27 bridge and at the roundabout cross the slip road, turning right. Keep on the pavement walking to the left into Vale Avenue. Turn right as signed to historic All Saints Church, Patcham and descend Church Hill to London Road. Turn left before the main road into Old London Road continuing past the shops and Memorial Hall across Ridgeside Avenue along The Woodlands. Before Elwyn Jones Court take the path down to continue along the pavement of London Road. The railway bridge giving access to Westdene is visible across the road up The Deneway.

At the bus stop after Carden Avenue head left into Withdean Park towards the seat and to the right of the copse behind it, heading to the gate in the fence. Continue up the park, gated for the benefit of dog walkers, through another gate up to a seat. Enjoy the scenic view west here from St Luke, Prestonville to the south across to Waterhall Mill (1885) in Patcham to the north. Turn left rising from the seat and walk beside the wood in front of the seats to Peacock Lane. Head left up to Braybon Avenue. Turn right. After Surrenden Crescent cross left to join the path on the wooded island in the centre of the dual carriageway. Continue right along this island, crossing with care various road junctions, as the carriageway bends left and continues down to its junction with Preston Drove.

Cross to the pavement left of St Mary's Catholic Church then over the zebra crossing and past the gate posts of Preston Park. Turn immediately right then left along the path between the hedges above the cricket pitch. Continue through the trees beside the car park and walk to the right of the terracotta Clock Tower (1892), left of the play area past the table tennis table to Rotunda Cafe and toilets. The walk heads right at the pond following around the rose garden. Head up the right hand steps and walk towards and then across the zebra crossing. Go immediately right across the next crossing then left along London Road. At the railway viaduct pause to look right and left into the sharply curved structure which has 27 arches and about 10 million bricks.

Head right along Argyle Road past the Argyle Arms pub (1866) up to New England Road. Turn right along the pavement under the metal bridge then right up the steps to enter Brighton Greenway passing the train model of Jenny Lind and the now decorative factory shed pillars. Cross Stroudley Road with care continuing up Greenway to the taxi rank roundabout. Proceed left of the cycle store into Brighton Station.

13.3 mile/21.3 km

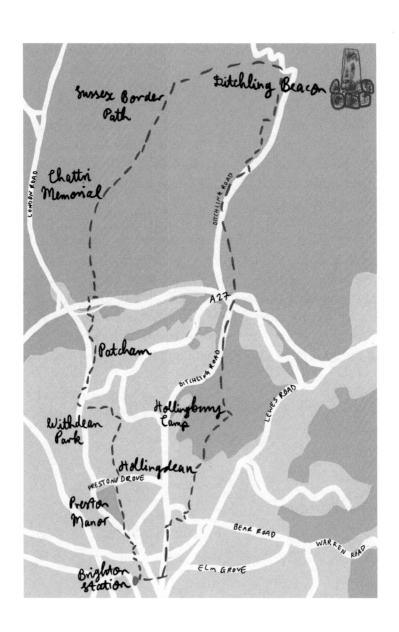

Sussex Border Path

Ditchling Beacon

Chattri Memorial

LONDON ROAD

DITCHLING ROAD

A27

Patcham

DITCHLING ROAD

Hollingbury Camp

LEWES ROAD

Withdean Park

Hollingdean

PRESTON DROVE

Preston Manor

BEAR ROAD

WARREN ROAD

Brighton Station

ELM GROVE

29   Telscombe

17 mile circular walk via Brighton Racecourse, Jugg's Road, South Downs Way to Telscombe returning via Under Cliff Walk

When streets are full of dust and noise, and all is heat and hurry here,
fresh memories of Sussex hills come to my mind with pictures clear...
There no one comes and all is still, save for the all untiring wind,
there with the long, dear waving grass, peace with the solitude I find.
Anonymous poem 'Retreat' (25)

Escaping Brighton's noise and hurry across the hills to Telscombe is indeed a 'retreat' coupled to a return journey along the Under Cliff walk. 'Telscombe is a civil parish and electoral ward (called East Saltdean and Telscombe Cliffs) with the status of a town in the Lewes District of East Sussex. It consists of three distinct settlements, separated from each other by an open area of downland called Telscombe Tye. Telscombe village... includes the parish church, with origins dating back to the 10th century. The village has a population of fewer than 50 people. The parish retains its ancient boundaries, which reach from the village to the coast, and the major part of the population is in the two coastal settlements. At the eastern end of the parish, about 4500 people live at Telscombe Cliffs... an extension of Peacehaven. At the western end, the remaining 2500 population forms part of the community of Saltdean, the remainder of Saltdean being within the city of Brighton and Hove. The Prime Meridian crosses the northeast corner of Telscombe parish... Although the ancient village of Telscombe is located less than two miles (3 km) from the coast, there is no public road linking the village with the coastal part of the parish. The byway was closed to all traffic in 2015. The village is found at the end of a winding dead end road leaving the Lewes-Newhaven road at Southease. All of which serves visitors on foot an especially peaceful walking circuit' (26).

Exiting the ticket barrier at Brighton Station turn left then left again past the cycle storage and taxi rank onto Stroudley Road. Descend the stairs and cross New England Street into Ann Street down to London Road. Cross into Oxford Street continuing across Ditchling Road into The Level heading diagonally left at the public toilets to the corner of the park. Cross Union Road and go straight ahead along Lewes Road past St Martin's Church. Cross the road and enter the Cemetery just before The Gladstone Pub. On Sundays the cemetery opens later at 11am. Continue towards Woodvale Crematorium following the road left up to Bear Road. Cross the road and turn right to walk up beside the City Cemetery walls. When you reach the top of Bear Road take the farm track to the left parallel to Warren Road which continues above Brighton Racecourse. After this becomes a cycle track, keep right at the junction and continue north of Woodingdean.

Cross Falmer Road with care into Drove Avenue to walk across the South Downs. At the junction after the telecommunications mast on Newmarket Hill keep right after which you enter the ancient Jugg's Road (track). After a short distance South Downs

Way (SDW) joins this track from the left and you leave Jugg's Road to head right along SDW. Enjoy views to the left of Lewes, Mount Caburn and the Radio Station above Glynde. SDW twists and turns heading upward to reveal a splendid view to the left of Seven Sisters and Seaford Head on the coastal horizon with Newhaven and Peacehaven radio mast to your right. SDW heads right then left onto a cemented track heading towards the striking Newhaven Energy Recovery Facility. Continue straight on SDW leaving the concrete road. After the signed path down to Rodmell village follow SDW down to the junction before the farm. Turn right along the bridleway leaving SDW and walk between the cattle sheds of South Farm. According to the farmer, the flattish field after the farm called Cricketing Bottom has crickets in season but may also have been used as a cricket green in the past. The walk continues in the same direction ignoring a right hand turn after which it passes left through a gate onto a path continuing to the right around a large field.

Go through the gate onto the road heading right in the same direction down into Telscombe village. Walk past Telscombe Manor with its round tower then square towered St Laurence Church with the Stud Farm opposite. Continue up to the cattle grid where the road ends. Head quarter right on the byway passing to the right of the pond to the left edge of the copse. The housing of Telscombe Cliffs and Peacehaven lie below to the left with Saltdean and Rottingdean to the right. Continue through the gate along the byway with Shoreham Power Station on the horizon. The path turns left along and then down Tennant Hill. After the transmitter descend Longridge Avenue past St Martin's United Reformed Church and the classic modern style Grand Ocean built as a luxury hotel in 1938 and the 'Stepping

Up' figurines (2013) beside it just off the road. Turn right at the bottom of the road across the pedestrian crossing and continue briefly along the South Coast Road towards Saltdean Lido.

Head left down the slope to the Under Cliff Walk which passes below the historic White Cliffs Cafe. Continue to Rottingdean beach, Ovingdean beach and then to the boatyard, pool and apartments of Brighton Marina. After passing the supermarket on your left, leave the Under Cliff Walk continuing straight up the slope under the road onto Madeira Drive. The walk continues on the promenade past the pier and crosses King's Road up West Street to the Clock Tower. Continue up Queen's Road to Brighton station.

16.7 mile/26.9 km

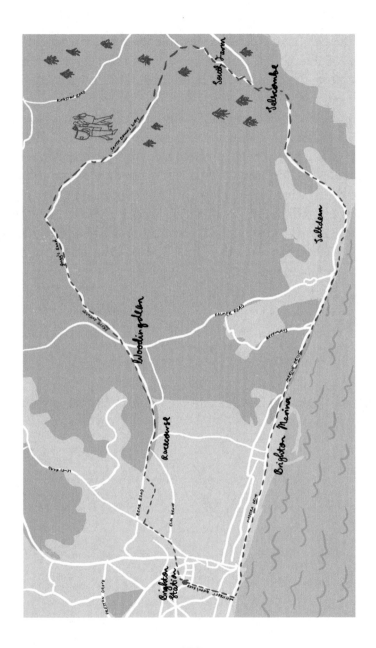

30   Truleigh Hill

18 mile walk via Devil's Dyke to Truleigh Hill returning via Southwick Hill and Shoreham Port

The view out to sea from Brighton to Worthing has been transformed in recent years by the construction of 116 windmill turbines 8 miles (13km) to 12 miles (20km) out to sea. Completed in 2018 Rampion Offshore Wind Farm (27) generates enough green electricity to power the equivalent of around 350,000 UK homes equivalent to half of the homes in Sussex. In recent years walkers from Devil's Dyke to Truleigh Hill and Steyning have seen a strip of laceration moving over the Downs, past Tottington Mount behind Truleigh Hill, appearing and then disappearing. This excavation was in conjunction with burying electric cables running to shore at Lancing from the wind farm, rising over the Downs and then descending to an electric substation at Twineham near Haywards Heath. Burying the cables was part of the agreement with the wind farm operatives to avoid a second set of pylons across the Downs, given the set that rises from Shoreham Power Station to Fulking Escarpment. This walk up to Devil's Dyke and along South Downs Way to Truleigh Hill passes under those cables and comes close to being over the wind farm cables under Tottington Mount. It presents scenic views south of the coast and wind farm and north across Mid Sussex.

From the ticket barrier at Brighton station continue straight ahead to the station forecourt and turn right. Cross the pedestrian crossing and turn right on the pavement up Terminus Road crossing before West Hill Tavern onto Howard

Place enjoying views to the right across Brighton. Brick built St Luke, Prestonville is on the horizon straight ahead. At Shakespeare's Head pub, cross Chatham Place continuing up Howard Terrace to Pentonville Road. Turn right enjoying the view from the bridge of the railway line to Hove then cross left into Russell Crescent walking to Good Companions pub on the junction. Turn right along Dyke Road and left across the pedestrian crossing at the junction with Old Shoreham Road (A270) by the Sixth Form College. Continue left on the pavement at the junction and cross the zebra crossing to walk alongside the playing fields which are accessible out of school hours.

After crossing Shirley Drive enter Hove Recreation Ground by the cafe and continue in the same direction on the path between the trees which exits onto the main road. Take a right turn immediately into the signed bridleway. Keep left at the path junction and continue to Goldstone Crescent. Cross into Monarch's Way which heads diagonally across family friendly Hove Park. Turn right at the climbing boulders and left before the miniature railway exiting the park up The Droveway past British Engineerium to cross Woodland Drive and ascend Nevill Road. Cross the zebra crossing to enter Court Farm Road passing St George's Roman Catholic Church. Before St Peter's Church, divert left down Holmes Avenue to view West Blatchington Windmill (c1820). Return to Court Farm Road, turn left past St Peter's and cross Hangleton Road at the crossing into Clarke Avenue.

Take the first right into Downland Drive which bends left to follow wooded access land. As the Drive bends left at the top head right into the signed pathway through the trees. After the sports ground the path descends to a T junction. Head right to cross the A27 over the footbridge. Continue straight ahead onto the metalled path which lies on an abandoned railway track and continue past West Hove Golf Course on your left. Just before Brighton & Hove Golf Clubhouse head left at the path junction and continue on the tarmac bridleway to Devil's Dyke Road. Cross the road and head left along the stone chip path to the road junction. Head across the road in the same direction onto a narrower path which runs parallel to the road up to Devil's Dyke Inn. On the ascent the road is traversed by the South Downs Way (SDW). Turn left through the metal gate continuing on SDW passing the trig point on your right. At the next gate SDW is joined by the path down from Devil's Dyke with its pub and viewing station, a possible detour.

Continue on SDW enjoying the view across Sussex and Surrey towards the North Downs and Fulking village below. After passing under the pylon-carried cables they walk heads over Fulking Escarpment to Truleigh Hill. The large radio transmitter has lesser acolytes that you pass before Truleigh Hill Farm. Turn left after the farm leaving SDW for the bridleway. Continue straight down enjoying the coastal view from the downs with Brighton & Hove to the left and Worthing and the Isle of Wight to the right. The path ascends Thundersbarrow Hill after which this walk's big staging post, Shoreham Power Station, looms on the horizon. At Southwick Hill which passes above the A27 road tunnel, continue straight ahead to the left of the sign and seat passing the trig point on your right. At the junction, continue straight to the right walking alongside the fence. The path descends past the 'Rest and be thankful' stone carried here as a boundary marker. This stone had previous service at St Michael & All Angels, Southwick but was made redundant by the building's enlargement in Victorian times.

The path ends at the top of Upper Kingston Lane. Continue down the lane past Quayside Youth Centre to Old Shoreham Road. Cross at the pedestrian crossing and continue straight down Kingston Lane passing the entrance to Shoreham Academy on the right. Turn left down Church Lane and continue past St Michael's Church to Southwick Green. Head half right passing to the right of The Cricketers pub into The Twitten. At the Ship Inn turn right along Station Road under the railway bridge adjacent to Southwick Station heading for the traffic lights on Albion Street. Turn right then cross the pedestrian crossing, which has an adjacent footpath sign, into the access road to Shoreham Port. Continue across the lock gates enjoying views of the River Adur ship canal under the towering edifice of Shoreham Power Station. Continue along Basin Road South and head across the zebra crossing onto the promenade. The walk can detour here to Shoreham Harbour.

Continue left along the promenade past Carat's Cafe and public toilets enjoying the sea view. The walk returns to Basin Road South for a stretch where you capture the commercial importance of the Harbour. There are opportunities to go back onto the sea walls and banks before the road bends left at the car park and right to Hove Lagoon. At the left turn head right off Basin Road South then onto the Promenade walking above the Lagoon past the beach huts. Enjoy the sea view continuing past public toilets to King Alfred Leisure Centre onto King's

Esplanade. There are public toilets off Hove Lawns as you continue to the Peace Statue. Continue past Brighton Beach Bandstand and the i360 viewing tower. The walk ascends up West Street to the Clock Tower and continues up Queen's Road back to Brighton Station forecourt.

18.1 mile/29.0 km

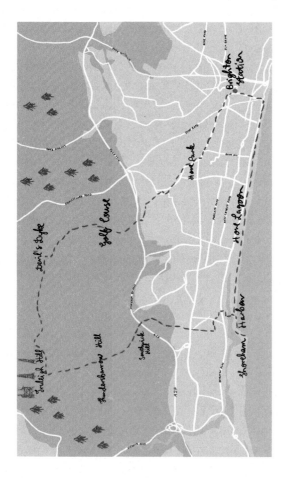

Notes

1   Colin Stephenson, Merrily on High (Canterbury Press, 1972) p23

2   St Bartholomew's Brighton, A Brief Guide (2021 pamphlet column 5)

3   Clifford Musgrave, Life in Brighton (History Press, 2011: first edition 1970) p263

4   Clifford Musgrave, Life in Brighton p150-1

5   Cuthbert Bede, Mattins and Mutton's or The Beauty of Brighton: A Love Story Vol II (London: Sampson Low, Son & Marston, 1866) p169

6   https://en.m.wikipedia.org/wiki/St._Ann%27s_Well_Gardens,_Hove

7   Derek Rogers, The History of Brighton in Brighton & Hove (SP Maps, 1996) p24

8   Clifford Musgrave, Life in Brighton p259

9   Details of the Stanford family on a display board at Preston Manor 2021

10   Clifford Musgrave, Life in Brighton p169, p174

11   https://en.m.wikipedia.org/wiki/Hollingbury

12   Clifford Musgrave, Life in Brighton p372-3

13   Derek Rogers, The History of Brighton p23

14   Clifford Musgrave, Life in Brighton p289-290

15   https://en.wikipedia.org/wiki/Brighton_and_Hove

16   https://en.wikipedia.org/wiki/Brighton_Racecourse

17   https://en.wikipedia.org/wiki/Lewes

18   Vera Arlett, Another Book of Sussex Verse edited C.F. Cook (Hove, Sussex Cambridge's, 1928) p219

19   Clifford Musgrave, Life in Brighton p345

20   Clifford Musgrave, Life in Brighton p354

21   http://www.tug-guide.com/english_guide/history.htm

22   https://steyningparishchurch.org/cuthman/

23   https://en.wikipedia.org/wiki/Monarch's_Way

24
https://www.historytoday.com/archive/natural-histories/how-did-elephant-get-its-trunk

25   Vera Arlett, Another Book of Sussex Verse p231

26   https://en.m.wikipedia.org/wiki/Telscombe

27   https://www.rampionoffshore.com/

About the author

John Twisleton is an ideas and people person, writer and broadcaster. He lives in Haywards Heath with involvements in London and Brighton. A Yorkshireman living in Sussex he now sees himself as much a Downsman as a Dalesman and is committed to lowering carbon footprints through recreational use of footpaths and public transport. He has published books on Horsted Keynes and prayer and is author of the popular 'Forty Walks from Ally Pally' and 'Fifty Walks from Haywards Heath'.

More at Twisleton.co.uk

Books by the Author

A History of St Giles Church, Horsted Keynes

Besides being the burial place of former UK Prime Minister Harold Macmillan (1894-1986) and mystic ecumenist Archbishop Robert Leighton (1611-1684) St Giles, Horsted Keynes has association with the history of Sussex back to the 8th century. As 53rd Rector (2009-2017) John Twisleton wrote this illustrated history with the assistance of church members.

Baptism - Some Questions Answered

Illustrated booklet on infant baptism used across the Anglican Communion. It explains the commitments involved in baptising a baby, challenges hypocrisy and attempts to clear up a number of misunderstandings in popular culture about what baptism is all about.

Christianity - Some Questions Answered

This booklet for Christian enquirers attempts dialogue between Christianity and its contemporary critics. A brief inspection of Christian faith clarifies both its unique claims and its universal wisdom so they can be seen and owned more fully.

Confession - Some Questions Answered

Illustrated booklet explaining the value of sacramental confession as an aid to spiritual growth. It commends confession as a helpful discipline serving people as they struggle against sin and guilt and seek to renew church membership.

Elucidations - Light on Christian controversies

As an Anglocatholic priest who experienced a faith crisis enlarging God for him, John Twisleton, former scientist, sheds light on thoughtful allegiance to Christianity in the 21st century condensing down thinking on controversial topics ranging from self-love to unanswered prayer, Mary to antisemitism, suffering to same sex unions, charismatic experience to the ordination of women, hell to ecology and trusting the Church, a total of twenty five essays.

Empowering Priesthood

This book is an enthusiastic presentation about the gift and calling of the ministerial priesthood. It argues that the choosing and sending of priests is vital to the momentum of mission and that their representation of Christ as priest, prophet and shepherd is given to help build love, consecrate in truth and bring empowerment to the whole priestly body of Christ.

Entering the Prayer of Jesus

Audio CD and booklet prepared by John Twisleton with the Diocese of Chichester and Premier Christian Radio providing spiritual wisdom from across the whole church. Contains audio contributions from Pete Greig (24-7 Prayer), Jane Holloway (Evangelical Alliance), Christopher Jamison (Worth Abbey), Molly Osborne (Lydia Fellowship) and Rowan Williams (Archbishop of Canterbury).

Experiencing Christ's Love

A wake up call to the basic disciplines of worship, prayer, study, service and reflection helpful to loving God, neighbour and self.

Against the backdrop of the message of God's love John Twisleton presents a rule of life suited to enter more fully the possibilities of God.

Fifty Walks from Haywards Heath

Sub-titled 'A handbook for seeking space in Mid Sussex' this book celebrates the riches of a town at the heart of Sussex. Through detailed walk routes with schematic illustrations John Twisleton outlines routes from one to thirteen miles with an eye to local history and replenishment of the spirit.

Firmly I Believe

Forty talks suited to Christians or non-Christians explaining the creed, sacraments, commandment and prayer engaging with misunderstandings and objections to faith and its practical expression. Double CD containing 40 easily digested 3 minute talks accompanied by reflective music with full text in the accompanying booklet.

Forty Walks from Ally Pally

John Twisleton explores the byways of Barnet, Camden, Enfield and Haringey with an eye to green spaces, local history and a replenishment of the spirit. The routes, which vary in length between one mile and twenty miles, exploit the public transport network, and are well designed for family outings. The author provides here a practical handbook for seeking space in North London.

Guyana Venture

The beauty and challenge of Guyana, formerly British Guiana, has drawn a succession of missionaries from the Church of

England to South America. 'Guyana Venture' is framed by John Twisleton's service there. Mindful of the ambiguities of the colonial past he writes proudly of the Church of England venture especially its helping raise up indigenous priests to serve Guyana's vast interior.

Healing - Some Questions Answered

An examination of the healing ministry with suggested ecumenical forms for healing services. The booklet addresses divine intervention, credulity, lay involvement, evil spirits and the healing significance of the eucharist.

Holbrooks History

Illustrated booklet compiled by John Twisleton with members of St Luke's Church, Holbrooks in Coventry about their parish and its church. It describes a multicultural community that has welcomed Irish, West Indian, Eastern European and Indian workers over the last century. The book includes dramatic pictures from the Second World War when the community and its church suffered bomb damage.

Meet Jesus

In a world of competing philosophies, where does Jesus fit in? How far can we trust the Bible and the Church? What difference does Jesus make to our lives and our communities? Is Jesus really the be all and end all? John Twisleton provides a lively and straightforward exploration of these and other questions pointing to how engaging with Jesus expands both mind and heart.

Moorends and its Church

Illustrated booklet telling the tale of the Doncaster suburb of Moorends from the sinking of the pit in 1904 to the 1984-5 mining dispute under the theme of death and resurrection. It includes a community survey of the needs of the elderly, young people and recreational and spiritual needs.

Pointers to Heaven

Completed at the height of COVID 19 this book condenses philosophical, theological and life insight into ten pointers to heaven troublesome to materialists: goodness, truth and beauty pointing to perfection alongside love, suffering, holy people and visions pointing beyond this world. If heaven makes sense of earth it is presented as doing so through such pointers, complemented by scripture, the resurrection and the eucharist, preview of the life to come.

Using the Jesus Prayer

The Jesus Prayer of Eastern Orthodoxy, 'Lord Jesus Christ, Son of God, have mercy on me a sinner' offers a simple yet profound way of deepening spiritual life. John Twisleton gives practical guidance on how to use it outlining the simplification of life it offers.

Printed in Great Britain
by Amazon

16278843R00099